Echoes
inside
the Labyrinth

Echoes
inside
the Labyrinth

Thomas McGrath

Thunder's Mouth Press • New York • Chicago

Published in the United States by Thunder's Mouth Press, Box 780, New York NY 10025 and Box 11223, Chicago IL 60611

Design by Laurie Bolchert

Grateful acknowledgement is made to the Illinois Arts Council and the National Endowment for the Arts for financial assistance with the publication of this volume.

Some of these poems have appeared in the following magazines: *Another Chicago Magazine, Beloit Poetry Journal, Cafe Solo, The Cat and the Moon, Chicago Review, Choice, Crazy Horse, Dacotah Territory, Far Point, Great River Review, Grove, Mainstream, Measure, Minnesota Review, The Nation, National Guardian, North Country, The Only Journal of the Tibetan Kite Society, Panama Gold, Poetry Now, Praxis, Refugee Journal, Rosinante, Sunbury Magazine, TriQuarterly, Uzzano, Voyages to the Inland Sea, We Sing Our Struggle, Willow Springs. Trinc* appeared in *The Ark #14* and in *The Pushcart Prize* (1980–1981 edition) and was published as a small book by Copper Canyon Press.

Some of the work on this book was made possible by grants from the NEA, the Minnesota State Arts Board, and the Bush Foundation. Thanks also to friends and students for help on some of these poems.

Library of Congress Cataloging in Publication Data

McGrath, Thomas, 1916–
   Echoes inside the labyrinth.

   I. Title.
PS3525.A24234E24   1983   811'.54   83-5056
ISBN 0-938410-13-X
ISBN 0-938410-12-1 (pbk.)

Distributed by
Persea Books
225 Lafayette St.
New York NY 10012

Contents

6. Echoes inside the Labyrinth

7. Passages

This book is for my brothers Martin and Joe, and my sister Kathleen; and for Tomasito

Trinc:

Praises II

Once, when the grand nudes, golden as fields of grain—
But touched with a rose flush like homeric cliches of dawn!—
Dreamed in prudential calm above the parochial lightning
Of bad whiskey;
           and when the contentious and turbulent General,
Handcrafted of fringed buckskin, legend, aromatic gunsmoke,
On the Greasygrass Little Bighorn lay down his long blond hair
At last at peace
          in his quiet kingdom
                  .   over the back-bar:
Then: the myth of Beer was born and the continental thirst!

O Beer we praise thee and honor thy apostolic ways!
Primero: for the glory of thy simple and earthy ancestors! As:
Instance: the noble Barley, its hairy and patriarchal
Vigor: golden
          in the windy lagers of manfarmed machine-framed fields;
Or in shocks or stooks
              tented
                like Biblical tribes
                    bearded
(But without the badrap of their barbaric god) gay,
Insouciant as encampments of the old Oglalla Sioux
Where each lodge opens eastward to the Land of the Morning Sun!

Praise for:
          segundo: the lacy and feminine elegance of the hops
Raising into the sun their herbal essence, medicinal,
Of the scent of the righttime rain fallen on rich earth.
They lift their tiny skirts—of Linnean Latin made!
Like those great nudes of the barrooms: souls of the newborn beer!

And we praise also Yeast: the tireless marine motors
Of its enigmatic enzymes, and its esters: like the submarine stars
Of astral rivers and horoscopic estuaries shining.

And we praise, last, the secret virtue of pure water,
A high lord among the Five Elements, gift of the heavens,
Its mineral integrity and the savor of secret iron!
Guitars are distilled from wine: from the politics of moonlight,
From the disasters of tequila and the edible worm in the deep well
Of mescal.
              But from beer comes banjos and jazz bands ecstatic
Trumpets midnight Chicago early thirties Bix.

It was Beer that invented Sunday from the long and salty days
Of the workday week:
                     that from the fast beer on horseback or the warm
Beer of the burning fields of the harvest, when the barley comes in,
Fermented the sabbatarian leisure;
                         that, in the eye of the workstorm,
For the assemblyline robotniki and the miner who all week long
Must cool his thirst at the root of the dark flower of the coal
Offered reprieve;
                  and for slow men on tractors (overalled
And perpetually horny) turned off their motors for the Sabbath calm.

It is farther from Sunday to Monday than to any other day of the week.
And Monday begins farther from home than a month of Sundays.
It begins in a deeper darkness than other days, and comes
From farther away, but swifter, to the sounds of alarums and whistles.
Six hours ahead of the sun it appears: first in dreams
Where we shudder, smelling the strength of sweat from the earlier east,
(Already at hard labor) and our sleep is filling with fireflies
From ancient forges, the hot sparks flying; then
It appears as grief for a lost world: that round song and commune
When work was a handclasp—before it built fences around us.

Monday is a thief: he carries in his weak and tiny fist
A wilted flower wrenched from our Sunday garden . . . still blue
With hope: but fast fading in the heat of his metal grasp.

Tuesday is born and borne like an old horse, coming
Home to the stall from the salt of the harvest fields, where, hitched
To sun and stubble, flyplagued and harness galled, sweatcrusted,
(The lather from under his collar whitening the martingales)
Teamed up he lugged the stammering machines through the twenty one-mile rounds
On the slowly narrowing field . . .
                                        Tuesday comes without flowers—
Neither Queen Anne's lace nor even Yarrow or Golden Rod—
(Most colorless of all the days of our week and work)
                                                without thunder,
(Like the old horse too tired to roll in the dust)
                                        without even
The anguish of Monday exile. It follows us home from our work.

Wednesday is born in the midweek waste like the High Sierra
Rising out of the desert, Continental Divide
In the long division of the septimal and sennight thirst;
                                                from where,
At Bridger's Pass or near Pike's Peak, at the last pine,
Cold, in the Wednesday snow, we halt for a moment and see:
Faraway, shining, the saltwhite glow of that Promised Land:
The Coast of Sunday—
                gold and maltgold—
                                        beyond Thursday's Mohave heat.

But Thursday is born in that mid-point halt at the hinge of the week
Where we seem too tired to push open the ancient five-barred gate
That lets on flowery holts and heaths and the faraway antic hay
Where leisure sprawls and dances in the fair of work-free fun . . .
Here thirst compounds his salty rectitudes: in Skinny Thursday:
That midweek Dog Day curse in Monday's cast-off shoes!

Friday is born in desperation, in the shadow of parables,
In the tent of Surplus Value, in the hot breath of Profit.
Yet it cometh forth as a fawn, yea as a young lamb
It danceth on prophetic mountains whose feet the Jordan laves!
Here is the time of the Dream Drinking, where our loves and needs
Come under the same roof-tree.
                            Evening of hope.
                                      Freer
Than manic Saturday and more adventurous than Sunday's calm.
Now we cast lots for our workweek clouts or put them in pawn!
And the night opens its enormous book wherein we invent our lives . . .

Saturday's children had far to go. We arrive as strangers
Entering the Indian Nation in the paycheck's prairie schooner,
Homesteaders in the last free land of the West . . .
                                      Already
The Sooners, those Johnny-Come-Earlies and claim jumpers
On the choicest barstools assert their squatter's rights . . .
They claim (these Dream Drinkers)—40 acres and a mule
Or a King Ranch bigger than all of Texas!
                                 It is Time they would
Reclaim from the burntout wagon train of the workweek waste.
Here each is Prince in his Castle Keep, but, outside, Time
Elaborates warp and woof and the ancient Enemies gather . . .
O blessed Beer, old Equalizer—doom for Commanches:
Shot down on Saturday's mesa in the flash of a 6 pack of Schlitz!

Deadflower, harness, halt-in-the-snow, dogday, holy hour!
By these five signs and passages we knew the laboring week
As we traveled and travailled toward Castle Keep, Compañeros Trabajeros!
And now, where Sundays buzz like flies caught in a web,
Drained of their workday strength, the golden spirit of Beer
Comes to lead us out of the net, if only a moment,
To where Possibility rolls out its secret roads
To picnic places where Potato Salad and the Olive and the Onion
And Ham-and-Cheese sandwiches position the kids on the grass;

Or to lazy creeks or lakes where the lunkers lounge and lunge,
Guides us;
        or into the popcorn smell and afternoon rituals
Of baseball fields shills us:
                where forever the high homer,
Smoking, of the great stars, writes their names on the sky . . .
And later, the firefly-lighted evenings, on back porches—
The vegetable lightning of those small stars caught in the grass . . .

Beer, birra, la biere, tiswin, pivo, cerveza—
In all its names and forms, like a polymorphic god, praise!
As, among Mexican stars and guitars: *Cresta Blanca*
And *Cuautemoc*: to be drunk under Popocatépetl
And Xochimilco;
        and *Fix*
             (named for Fuchs) in Greece,
Either in Ammonia Square where the poor go or in Syntagma
Where the umbrellas gather the bourgeoisie in their shade;
And *San Miguel* where the Philippines offer expendable chickens;
And *Heinekin* cold as the Hans Brinker canals where the Dutch
Are skating around on tulips and wooden shoes; and *Pilsener*
Resurrected from Nazi and allied bombings, old-world gold,
Of the Czechs and Slavs;
        and all the melodious beers of Spain;
And of England, land of the mild and bitter: *O'Keefe's* and *Watney's Ales*;
And, of Ireland, *Guinness Stout* with its arms of turf and gunfire;
And Australia's *Melbourne Bitter* from way down under!

Beer which passes through vats like the multiple stomachs of ruminants
To be lagered in sunken cloisters in monkish gloom till the day
When, on the brewery dray, it is ceremonially borne
Through the sunny morning towns by those great and noble beasts
Those horses with necks of thunder and fetlocks like hairy paint brushes.

Beer of Milwaukee! Beer of St. Louis! Where Lewis and Clark
Passed in the days of the furtrade and the wide ranging voyageurs.
And pass still, like ghosts, day after day, unseen
And forgotten: still hunting that West that was lost as soon as found—
Legends in search of a legend:
                                        As the new beers of the West
Lucky and *Lone Star*, *Olympia*, *Grain Belt*, *Coors*
Seek the phantom perfection of the mythic beers of the past!

Beer, not to be sipped but lifted against the palate—
Like the mystical cargo of argosies: lofted into the holds
Where the hideaway ports of the Spanish Main set their top-gallants
To drag their island-anchors into the New World!

Comestible beer that puts the hop in the Welsh Rabbit!
Beer-soup-du-jour that causes the cheese to sing!
Beer that transmogrifies the evening's peasant pot roast!
That metamorphizes the onion in the Sunday carbonade!

Praise, then, for *pulque* and *kvass*, for *chang*, for *weissbier*
For *suk* and *sonshu*, for *bousa* and all the hand-me-down
Home brews!
                    No firewater, aqua forte, blast-head or forty-rod
But heart medicine: made for fast days or fiesta:
For the worker in his vestments of salt at the end of our laboring days,
Or for corroboree and ceilidh where the poem sings and says:
Praise for the golden liquor of Wakan Tanka or god!
Praise for its holy office—O offer hosanna and laud!
By sip, by sup, by tot, by tipple, by chuglug—*all* ways:
Hallelujah! For the People's Beer! And for all His comrades: praise!

Some Years 2

Winter Roads

In the spring thaw
The winter roads over the cold fields
Disappear
In front of the last sled.

All summer they sleep
Hidden and forgot
Under the green sea of the wheat.

Now, in autumn,
They rise
Suddenly
Out of the golden stubble.
They arch their backs in the sun
And move slow and crooked across the fields
Looking for winter.

Beyond The Red River

The birds have flown their summer skies to the south,
And the flower-money is drying in the banks of bent grass
Which the bumble bee has abandoned. We wait for a winter lion,
Body of ice-crystals and sombrero of dead leaves.

A month ago, from the salt engines of the sea,
A machinery of early storms rolled toward the holiday houses
Where summer still dozed in the pool-side chairs, sipping
An aging whiskey of distances and departures.

Now the long freight of autumn goes smoking out of the land.
My possibles are all packed up, but still I do not leave.
I am happy enough here, where Dakota drifts wild in the universe,
Where the prairie is starting to shake in the surf of the winter dark.

History

All night the wind
Yelled at the house,
The trees squeaked and hushed
But the wind would not.
All night the trees complained
And the rain rushed and rained.

Now in the cool
Morning the trees stand, tall,
Still and all composed—
Sun on their sunny pages.
Of the storm only the riled
Creek remembers; and rages.

Autumn Song

Autumn has emptied heaven of its birds
And stretched a silence on the loud sea.
Gone is the last leaf and the last flower,
And all the gauds of summer are undone.

     Winter cuts off our feet. But we must dance
     In Spring's conspiracy of circumstance:
     Swallows sickling air's invisible grass
     Sketch hieroglyphs that translate at a glance
     To greenest meaning.
                        The sun, love's looking-glass,
     Summer, that stokes the furnance of the bee,
     Honey all nature in one grand romance—
     The ambience of consanguinity
     Hurls its huge myth around the world at me.

But now the sports and sunny shows are done.
A deadflower clock ticks out a year of seed.
The season's losses hide the summer road,
And crows talk hoarsely in the frozen wood.

At Fargo

The down trees,
Over the winter ice,
Still hold the scalps of last year's high water.

A hundred yards from my house—
Across the Red River—
The beavers are gnawing the Minnesota dark.

Spiritual Exercises

I fed on flesh until
That honey was bitter as gall;
Then grew drunk on the soul's
Lightning and alcohol.

Now flesh and soul both stink.
Lightning and honey pall.
Bitter grows sweet at last
And laughter is all.

Song

When I was terrible and young
The world was ravishing and wild.
And randy as the day was long,
I loved it quietly and cold.

Now I am sober, old and sane
And the wild world is cool and tame;
Time freezes at my finger tip—
But now my love grows hot and quick.

Love Belongs to the North

It is true.
        Consider the wild duck
                the trumpeter
Swan
    that high arrow of feathers and flesh cutting
The moon
        those mystical wranglers on their ladders of ice.

How, far from the south they fare
                over the noon angle!
                      Lift
The tropical furnaces of their bodies
             dark fire in their bones
From the quacking sensual swamp
           blood's ease
               turn away.

Farewell now to the South! Choir and arc strung
Singing to meet the spirit on its high trapeze in cold zones
Fiery where the deep North mates the meridians of flesh and wish.

There to endorse the history of the blood in that landscape of love.
There, in pine barren
          tundra
            frozen estuary
Cold glacial river milky among reeds
              where they come in.
To sing the essential solitary note.

The Dreams of Wild Horses

Night and full moon.
A profane rhythm of
Man-throwing unsanctified broncos
Stampedes like wildfire
Into the sin-colored badlands.

Here, nightlong they invent new names,
Christening themselves
In the cold creek.
The dawn sky expells
Their lunar voices.

Harnessed to sunlight,
Sowing the city of silence,
They plant their names
In the dark.

Crazy Horse is dead.
Parched buffalo bones.
Moonlight weathering in the dry corn.

Weather Report

When I came up out of the well,
I saw the *weather*!

The stars were brighter down there,
But here's a cloud no bigger than a John Deere tractor,
(In fact it *is* a John Deere tractor)
And here is a blizzard in the form of a self-propelled combine,
And that low going out to the north to let in the polar air
Is sixteen bundle-teams and a spike-pitcher.

When I came up out of the well,
Everyone was drinking moonshine.
From the junkyard, ancient Ford cars come snuffling
Like hound dogs: coon-trails, lost roads—flowers in their nostrils . . .
The barometer is full of ancient machinery stuffed with flowers
McCormack reapers, hammers and sickles, *Hupmobiles*! *Orchids*!
How in the *hell* can it rain?

Time Zones

for Tomasito

I see you there in a blaze of sun, little son
Where the waters of the Pacific are at your feet.
Here, the light has gone out of the snow;
I watch you out of a darkness
That gathers from somewhere beyond the Dakota sundown.

Another Day

The morning
Uncoils
Out of a cloud of light—
The whole east pearly
With the milk of nativity
As if the world were being born again
Just over the hill.

The animals pin their shadows
Against the sky.
The birds tug at the sun.
And in this dawn
It seems that water might run uphill
As the new day bears into the world on its back
A tree of light like splendor lifted from Eden
While the morning
Uncoils.

And does it rattle?

It rattles.

The Old McGrath Place

The tractor crossed the lawn and disappeared
Into the last century—
An old well filled up with forgotten faces.
So many gone down (bucketsful) to the living, dark
Water . . .
        I would like to plant a willow
There—waterborne tree to discountenance earth . . .
But then I remember my grandmother:
Reeling her morning face out of that rainy night.

Tantara! Tantara!

We come home to the wild garden in the first of the autumn fevers.
An ax of bright frost has levelled the high flowers,
And the horse of the northwest wind has ridden them into the ground.

All sensitivities are undone, the round weave of the summer.
Only the proletarian cabbage reclaims in its mellow
Heart the cold promise of the early rain crow, only
The vulgar squash has hurdled the fence—its rasping trumpets, its
Yellow hounds sounding.
                                And the pigs run squealing to the woods.

Salute

Something has punched a hole in the afternoon . . .
Thunder, perhaps.
Later, the rain.

—And a mysterious history of accidental artifacts
In the testimentary ditches of the drifting city:
Restless wooden legs walking on water,
Hungry manifestoes half eaten
Roses at the point of maximum entropy
Second mortgages on back-lots in the moon . . .
Postcards, postcards condoms wish you were here
Postcards postcards postcards.

At the end of it all,
A shy girl, dancing in the drenched light,
Collects,
In her wet unquenchable curls,
A piece of the true gold sun
From the dark, cold deep
Of the sky.

Toward Paradise

Outside my window the apple trees lift
The terrible weight of their fruit
Effortlessly. Or so it seems.
And the apples round and ripen
In a timescale slower than mine.
There is comfort and terror
In this grace, this patience.

Go Ask the Dead 3

Go Ask the Dead

1

The soldier, past full retreat, is marching out of the grave
As he lies under dying grass in the slow judgment of time
On which he has lost his grasp.

                                        And lost his taste as well—
For, tell-tale as fast as it will, no tongue can put salt on his name.
The captain sun has done with this numberless underground.

2

He has seeded out of that flesh where the flashing lights first fade
In the furry sky of the head.

                     And the orient admiral brain
Has seen its images go like ensigns blown from a line—
Those raving signals.

                         All quality's bled from his light,
And number (he's all thumbs now) divides where infinities fail.

3

Grand winds of the sky might claim; or the blue hold
Of ocean accept;

               or fire sublime—

                        though it's earth
Now hinders and halters

             him.

                    But those underground birds, his bones,
(Homeless all havens save here) fly out of their low-hilled heavens
And shine up into the light to blaze in his land's long lie.

4

And long they lie there but not for love in the windy contentions
Of sun and rain, shining. This endless invasion of death
Darkens our world. There is no argument that will move them.
"You are eating our light!" they cry. "Where have you taken the sun?
You have climbed to the moon on a ladder of dead man's bones!"

Fresco: Departure for an Imperialist War

They stand there weeping in the stained daylight.
Nothing can stop them now from reaching the end of their youth.

Somewhere the Mayor salutes a winning team.
Somewhere the diplomats kiss in the long corridors of history.

Somewhere a politician is grafting a speech
On the green tree of American money.

Somewhere prayer; somewhere orders and papers.
Somewhere the poor are gathering illegal arms.

Meanwhile they are there on that very platform.
The train sails silently toward them out of American sleep,

And at last the two are arrived at the very point of departure.
He goes toward death and she toward loneliness.

Weeping, their arms embrace the only country they love.

Remembering the Children of Auschwitz

We know the story. The children
Are lost in the deep forest—
Though it is the same forest
In which we all are born.

But somehow it has changed:
A new kind of darkness,
Or something they never noticed,
Has colored the pines and the larches.

And now appears the Bird,
(Bird of a strange dreaming)
To lead them, as tales foretold,
Over the little streams

Into the garden of order
Where trees no longer menaced,
And a little house was protected
Inside its candy fences.

And all seemed perfectly proper:
The little house was covered
With barbwire and marzipan;
And the Witch was there; and the Oven.

Perhaps they never noticed—
After all that disorder
Of being lost—that they'd come
To the Place named in the stories.

Perhaps there was even peace—
A little—after disorder,
Before they awoke into
A dream of deeper horror.

And now the Bird will never
Take them across the river
(Though they knew how to walk on water).
They become part of the weather.

They have become the Ascensions.
When we lift up our eyes,
In any light, we see them:
Darkening all our skies.

Higher Criticism

The spirit is in love with beauty—so the philosophers tell us.
And the poets, a bit absent-minded, agree, counting their breaths.
The artist nods, complacent, blowing his abstract nose,
Framing a wornout mattress to hang in the new museum.

Meanwhile injustice fills the street like tear-gas,
Covers the city in a lachrymal fog, seeps in
Through the broken windows of the poor houses
And muffles the cries of children with the stench of modern times.

The poet is on vacation and cannot smell it.
To the philosopher it is the-merely-contingent—
A quantum of the necessary friction in the *ding-an-sich*.
The painter has got it somehow mixed in with his paints,

And lolloping and lallygagging by go the lucky ones who have learned
To correct their vision from dolors to sense—*Aurea! Aurea!*
The poor look in at *that* strange world through the lens of a tear
Made in the factories they work in and ground by themselves to fit . . .

Still: the fumes condense on the windows of endowed academies.
The acid invades the bindings of all the Summas.
It is this which corrodes the silver of Pulitzer Prizes
And rusts all the paint in the Museum of Modern Art.

The Lineaments of Unsatisfied Desire

1

The new President wants—and pronto!—
Some heavy metal to drop south of the border.
G. M. demands an invasion of Cuba or anywhere—
On a cost-plus basis.
The League of Labor Fakers desires only
Class-collaboration and injunctions against strikes.

2

Nevertheless, Big Bill Haywood has planted the Red Flag
On Alpha Centauri. And Rosa Luxembourg
Has placed in permanent orbit the Communist Manifesto.

3

The stock market rises or falls in hot pursuit
Of the perennial mechanical rabbits of misery and money.
But, in Hazard, Kentucky, the coal is, again,
Slyly invading the earth.

The Histories of Morning

Morning spells light in the language of alarm clocks.
The streets bulge with ambition and duty—
Inhaling the populace out of exhausted houses.
The drowsy lion of money devours their calendars
In an absent-minded orgy of universal togetherness.

Meanwhile back among the ranch-type ramblers
The television set loosens the apron strings
Of housewives temporarily widowed
By that same quotidian lion of hard labor.

Now they are carried away by bowlegged heroes
To covered-wagon livingrooms of the openfire range:
Where the Masked Man turns out to be an old lover.

Somewhere—in the kitchen—the coffee is chuckling like Pandar.
Somewhere the factories shake in the fists of the workers.

Jazz At The Intergalactic Nightclub

The management is pleased to announce:
That as a result of the recent elections to the Universal
                            Congress of Transmogrification,
There will be revelations . . . visions . . . charismatic hors-
                        d'heuvres . . . mana . . . divine grace . . .
Exactly at midnight;

And is further pleased to advise you
That every instant of time this bright dark long,
No matter what the time-belt of your home province,
Shall be that true and enduring midnight,
This eternal heaven in which we dream of hell.

Look at the clock, ladies and gentlemen:
It is three seconds until that ultimate midnight,
That Universal Prime, moment of Grace, final rent payment,
                            Revelation, Satori,

Three . . .
Two . . .
One . . .

There.
It has happened.

Now you may all go home.

Dopers' Song at Little Ah Sid's

(from a play in progress)

How would you like to forget your woes?
At Little Ah Sid's anything goes.
You can kick the gong around and kick it again,
Down in your friendly neighborhood opium den.

You can forget your quarrels with the boss and with god—
Till Kingdom Come you can stay on the nod!
You can smoke it, shoot it, or stick it up your ass—
Whichever way you do it it's always a gas.

You may think it's cold when you're not on the hop—
Well the ice-age cometh and the snow will never stop.
If you're feelin' down and dirty and you're all alone,
Come in out of the weather and we'll all get stoned!

Gotta get all your shit together—
Stick it in your arm against bad weather!
Come on inside in the early snow,
And we'll all be swingin' when the wagons go!

Ho ho honey, have a whiff on me,
Have some uppers have some downers have some boo have some tea!
It's a drag to stay straight stay stoned instead—
'Cause when the Boss Junky gets ya yer a long time dead!

Song: Miss Penelope Burgess, Balling the Jack

Barefaced baby with the three minute dream
Waking at morning with a soundless scream—
Not another ace in the dream-rigged packs,
Nothing but jokers and the non-wild jacks;

Oh baby, baby, when the light breaks clean
(And there's nothing to run on but a benzedrine)
It's back on the bricks and hustle the stem
Where the buffalo are thicker than the iron men.

Git it up, give it up, I hear you cry.
But one day and another and life goes by,
A little bit lousier day by day
But at last at last at last at last it's all gone away—

Then it will come easy, when there's nothing to lose,
Nothing to hope and nothing to choose,
No reason to cry, no reason to sing
Just nothing, nothing, nothing, nothing—

Oh, I hear you crying, baby, in your platform shoes,
With your Cadillac mutant or your cut-rate booze;
I hear you in your brogans or in sable or mink
Where the clubwomen chatter or the chippies swink.

Was it Prince Charming who deceived you from the age of ten
And threw you on the town in the world of men?
Did you look for honor and discover its lack
As you struggled for power from flat on your back?

Was it the books that tricked you or the priests that lied—
Promising, promising equality and pride,
While the boss demanded profit and the husband wanted more—
A dual purpose property both mother and whore?

We all helped to make you and the way you are:
Signed with our dishonor, an invisible scar.
Dream bitch-goddess, or terrible nurse,
On all of us who've harmed you I call down a curse.

Long gone lady with your three minute dream
Waking in a trap with a soundless scream
(As the child will scream at the terror of birth)
Where will be born your dignity and worth?
In what new heaven? On what different earth?

Revolutionary Song

Under America's glittering darkness
Assemble the armies of finks and narcs
Who poison the daylight. What's to be done?
Sell all you have and buy a gun!

    What shall we do with the Pope of Racine?
    With the Witch and the Shaman of the ancien regime?
    Can St. Marx defend us from their spells and black masses
    And cast a rebel I-Ching up their asses?

With tumbrel and timbrel and dynamite-psaltry
We'll confound the Congress-of-Gold gestalt.
When the Carpetbaggers Trust goes broke
We will socialize Charity, Faith and Hope!

    Will we know enough to plug the sorcerers?
    Shoot at the whites of their eyes or their auras?
    We will lower the barometer and call up storms
    Against feathermerchants, weathercocks and bourgeois charms!

Only the workers shall remain
When the Black Maria of Time comes round.
Brother, insure that the time will come—
Sell all you have and buy a gun!

The Homilies of Bedrock Jones

Though all the navies of the world
Could float in proletarian sweat,
The capitalist magician can
Walk round the Horn and not get wet.

While Nature's fruits are offered up
As bounty for the common good,
The fastidious bourgeois hoards them all
And dines on the workers' body and blood.

And priest and teacher alike conspire
To prove as natural of divine
A system where labor feeds the sloth,
They bless the criminal, hallow his crime.

By the logic of this philosophy
Bankers are wrapped in the grace of God
While the windows of the workers' minds
Are lapped by a cold and ignorant fog.

Yet through those windows light does come
And consciousness creates a face
As brother fingers invent a fist.
Irrepressible conflict must

End in the endless work of peace:
The commune of the "toiling masses"—
Or, as Marx explained, "in the
Mutual ruin of contending classes."

Cool Hand Kelly Pleads Extenuating Circumstances

I'm a lazy intemperate man, sentenced to hard labor.

No time for leisure

No time for love

No time for the Revolution

But it isn't *just* because I have cold hands

That I was condemed

       to read

Each bit of news

       printed

On every snowflake

       that falls

In all the winters that come.

Ghost Talk

Yeah, I know what they say . . .
Everybody thought I had it so good out there—
Forest Lawn . . . right over near the Wee Kirk of the Heather
—real white-ghost country.

But those damn bells never stop!
And that grave! Too long or too short—one.
And the roots of the trees always changing their shoes!
I rose like a heat-seeking missile
From the rocket-launcher of my terrestrial connection.

But now, friends, I want to go back to sleep again.
Up here I get sun-stroke, moon-stroke, water-stroke.
I want to go back where the dark ain't so full of holes.
Anybody got a heaven-caliber dream-pistol handy?

At the Edge of the Glacier

It looks sullen, sleeping in its stony bed,
Like someone determined to be sick forever.
Its color is not the color of any homegrown ice,
But pale. Cadaverous. The color of ice in a reefer where a hobo died.

In its Other Life it is barreling down the mountain
At the speed of an express train in Switzerland, perhaps, where they have such trains.
The sun, riding in the observation car, is blue with cold
And its teeth are jagged and shattered
Like those of an old lion who tried to devour all Africa.

In its cold dream the glacier is dropping its calves
Ten thousand miles south in the Brazillian wheatfields.
As it smokes through the slow stations,
It sweeps-up the stationmasters, their pots of zinnias,
Morning papers and timetables. All the compartments are full.

Here comes the New Age Limited! All aboard!

The Poet of the Prison Isle: Ritsos Against the Colonels
for Carolyn Forché

So there you are,
Jannis Ritsos,
On that island of pure salt
Where it only rains on the dead.

. . . .

Statues of sand statutes
Of gall
Enormous legends of the Platonic Republic founded on gunpowder.

Hush
The Colonels are coming
The King is Coming
Tra La

. . . .

Meanwhile you are dying. And harder than in any poem.
Of course we are all trying to keep the frontiers open people are doing desperate things
    to save you some people read the times and are indignant some people read the past
    and are indignant some madwoman is reading her personal memoirs personally over
    WEVD explaining the values of those who put you out there the first time.
All's ordnung as Ez sez and let's not forget the poets carefully writing in lowercase and
    erasing if they hit a capital.

. . . .

Well, there are damn few capitols where they might want you
Outside the revolutionary world.
I guess
The poets and all being what they are you'll die where you're at.

A sad thing
Because you are the only one in the world who heard
Those terrible trains in the heads of widows
The trains that carry the conscripts
To that bosses' war—the one
Just over the border.

In the Sleep of Reason

The pilot, returned, sees the village
Unwrap itself
            in slow motion
Releasing its nameless people into history,
On film.

          But he is still up there,
Dreaming,
With his toy gun
Lying in the high grass
At 40,000 feet.

Any Day Of The Week: A Sunday Text

Where Bourgeois Right lays ambushes
With pigging string and hooleyann,
He catches those already caught.
My lasso's for a wilder man—

One who, though roped both hand and foot,
Roves at large, boundless and free.
Travellers maintain there are such ones;
But in another, far, countree.

Psalm: El Salvador

1. All the landscapes are accelerating:
2. The sun is drowning, but the doors of the sea are open to formal logic.
3. I.E.: salt, garlic, the transcendental shoes of the beggar.
4. Starlight doesn't pay for the work of the miners.
5. The dogs have scared the daylights out of the moon . . .
6. The reason the snow is sad is that the rabbits have no shoes.
7. Maybe if there was less silence we would talk more?
8. Maybe if there were more noise we would talk more. . . .
9. Awls. Mauls. Small clothes. Empire balls.
10. Supposing you want?
11. Supposing you want *more*?
12. The shoes of the poor always have one stone in them.
13. Houses of the rich. Flood. Fire. And the dreams of Anarchists.
14. The sun does not pay for the work of the miners.
15. All the landscapes are slowing down.
16. Formal logic invented the sea.
17. Especially the waves.
18. And that drowned fisherman now being washed up on shore.
19. Moonlight will not pay the widow's rent.
20. Perhaps it is time we should all go to Acapulco?
21. The beach is the shit-house of the sea.
22. Supposing you want less?
23. Fire, star, sea, sun, stone,
24. And, if necessary, a little coffee— or perhaps: saphires.
25. Let's!
26. Why not?
27. Harpies vampires ghouls zombies bankers lawyers and *paper*.
28. Snow doesn't pay for the work of the miners.
29. Just suppose . . .
30. And the rabbit of course and the snow
31. Underground, the miner and the fisherman are at home in the same earth.
32. Will you visit my finca?
33. Let's!
34. Let's not.
35. Will you visit my latafundia?

36. Let's!
37. Why not?
38. The wind does not pay rent for the fisherman's widow
39. Bile black bile green bile yellow bile red bile
40. Of course. of course, as they say.
41. Here come the guerillas!
42. Let's get a tight close up of the leader:
43. Perhaps you would like to visit my finca?
44. I would like to visit your latafundia.
45. The rabbit really has shoes and the snow is not so sad.
46. Let us visit the house of the widow of the dead fisherman
47. And the widow of the dead miner.
48. And the dead guerilla. And the dead
    Poet
    Nun
    Child
    Dog
    Moon
49. The Chase Manhattan Bank does not pay for the work of the dead.
50. Think of the beautiful things
51. I am thinking:
    Rabbit shoes
    Machine guns
    Grenades
    The dead
    guerilla
    The moon
52. *Take it down*
    Take it ALL down
53. I am thinking of the dead guerilla.
54. I am thinking of the dead guerilla.
55. I am thinking of the dead guerilla.
56. I am thinking of the dead guerilla.
57. ¡ ! ¡ ! ¡ ! ! !

Visions of the City 4

Visions Of The City

I Morning

You are aware of the weather first of all, and the limits of the known world, the sign of the Army and Navy Store on the Avenue, or, from the fifteenth story, the line of mist out toward Staten Island. The light is clean and new, not yet soiled by the commerce of the day. Over the Bronx there is a small lost cloud, unable to go anywhere in the dead still air. In Jackson Heights, the last apple falls from the tree. On a street in Hoboken a tenement wall collapses and the dust is puffed up into the clean light. Up and down. The world is arranging its weights and measures.

A million workers charge down the dusty chutes of the cold-water apartment houses, are siphoned off and sucked away into the subways. The bottom has fallen out of the barometer of sleep. Adjustments are made: in the fur district the pressure of industry is rising; and through the fog of brick and stone, over the steel bones of the skyscrapers down-town, you see the thin red line of humanity and profit rise in exact ratio to the falling line on sleep's soiled glass. Up and down.

When you go into the street, history begins. The headlines tie your hands and put you against the wall; or they arm you with little bottles of blue vitriol and tell you when to throw. Civil war in Indo-China. Starvation in Puerto Rico. Third day of the longshore strike. You are beyond the limits of the visible world now. You begin to move in other dimensions, but it is not too late to turn back, for you, the neutral man, the housewife on the Grand Concourse where the Bronx dreams on its seventeen hills, the man on the fifteenth floor looking at the line of haze toward Staten Island, or the caretaker of the C.Y.O. The strike, the civil war, do not involve the neutral man; they do not affect the weather or the qualities of the light which the headlines collect and flash black as the leaves on the tree in the little playground just down Seventeenth Street from Eighth Avenue flash green. You are aware, back safely within the visible world of objects, that it is a green day, although it is October, and the leaves are falling and are not really green at all. Nevertheless Central Park is the green of an island in a calm morning sea. The underside of the leaves is paler, the green of barn paint mixed with milk. If you are sleeping on one of the park benches, this green is the color of the world when you wake. If you are a bartender, the green of the neon is that of a watergauge filled with fishblood. At Red Hook, a harbor policeman, you snatch a three-day-old corpse out of the water, and around his fingernails you see the dirty green of moss in an unused chimney.

But you see that the green is changing, and in the street the world of solid objects is taking on motion as the morning progresses. Nothing is constant. At fifteen stories up, the quantity of cosmic rays per square inch per second striking your body differs from the rate at which they are bombarding the corpse at sea level. The streets are changing, taking on a new character, as people rush onto the metal runways and the subways race away to remote frontiers around Bath Beach and Pelham Bay. The city of sleep disintegrates, the crystal atom is smashed, and the components are tearing away at different velocities, outward and away. The tunnels clog with cars, a ship mourns, laboring toward Cape Hatteras, and three boys, none of them more than twelve years old, catch an empty on the New York Central on the first leg of their westward trip to Pueblo just as the third flight for Shannon Airport and Europe glints like a sliver of ice in the sun over Long Island.

Everything is dissolving, breaking up, racing away, trying to be free. You recognize the same desire in the people in the street. They have the light of hallucination in their eyes, and like maniacs driven by their own obscure compulsions they move in straight lines, bumping into each other, knocking each other down without ever looking at what they have hit. Like the light which touched the top of the Empire State Building early this morning, and which is now charging out toward the limits of space at a constant speed, they are propelled along invisible rails by a planless mechanics.

You do not have to think of them as human, because you are the neutral man. Even though they have this desire to be free, it is only an aspect of disintegration, movement away from the center, like the desire for liberty in the heart of a stick of dynamite. You see them pass on the street: blind, hurried, driven. In the Bronx you see the fanatical hitchhikers staring up the burning highway through the map of Maine. Off Red Hook the tides deposit the corpse on your grappling hook as surely as the sides of beef are hooked on the overhead trolleys along Fourteenth Street. And down toward the docks you see a small man with black hair and a bundle of leaflets under his arm, flung outward from the mass like a new moon not yet cooled or hardened, moving in a moving nimbus which is his unconsidered desire to be free.

II Noon and Afternoon

You hear the bells of daylight scatter their iron command-ments over the city and a ragged cloud of pigeons circles from the fountain near the park. Blue-white, stone-color, glove-soft pinions, they break up like spray on a rock and explode in every direction across the high clear sky. There appears to be no pattern there, nor along the sidewalks where, like ant-streams following a corridor of scent, people turn off into the sweetpockets of the banks or the dime-stores. The river breaks up before the pool is made; the winner comes home before the betting machines are installed; unbalanced equa-tions. You observe the rivers running crazily in circles around the island, the bridges turn to all compass points, and the bus comes down the street with no driver at the wheel. Neverthe-less, patterns are taking form.

You note the pattern in the golden dust where the pigeon tracks end in air and sunlight. The iron hours fall from the bells onto the bedunged, shining roofs of the city, different and alike. The pigeons scatter, coalesce, circle and return to the fountain as weightless as pollen. You begin to be aware of the patterns of the day.

The first is the pattern of disintegration when the sunrise gun shatters the fortress of sleep. Crazed with breakfast cof-fee and the pangs of necessity, the people begin their vast migrations. They charge through the early streets as mad as elephants in the season of *must*. The doors of offices reach out for them; they fall into the great pitfalls of the factories; in the enormous wells of the elevator shafts imprisoned prophets mourn in vain. A hundred suicides wearily climb the great cliffs of the highest buildings and fall, timing themselves, perfectly evenly spaced and shining like meteors, onto the iron plateaus of the avenues. Statisticians in frockcoats rush out to determine the amount of scatter, checking against curves.

Under the glass dome of noon you see everything become fixed, static again. In the doze of midday, life is coming back again into the fur and garment districts, into the lofts of the chemical and radio industries. Workers sleep or sit in the sun at the entrances to garages and shipping departments. This is the happiest hour of the day, an hour in which there is no work, an hour too short to start the climb to Golgotha in search of amusement. The denim jackets and the work shirts gather the warmth and the sunlight of a perfectly free hour, the time when no one works or worries about being happy. You know, of course that it cannot last. Sunlight spills from the blue jackets as the one o'clock whistle whirls them into activity; the curse of progress falls like a meteorite on a glass roof and the workers climb the burning stairs to the cave mouth, shoot up in the stalactite-hung elevator-shaft, jet propelled, to the seventhousand story entrance to the hornacle mine where the mad scientist is waiting with his tiresome plan for minting ten dollar bills out of their blood.

That is the end of the pattern of repose, and it is the only one of the day.

At six o'clock another pattern emerges. It is at that time, when the air is blue with exhaustion and the whole city barely manages to stand on its steel and stone foundations, the girders almost eaten through with fatigue and hatred, the bridges swaying drunkenly, their foundations sapped by malaise and industrial insanity; then, in the blue hour, when the bosses know enough not to come around, because since four o'clock every worker has been sharpening his knife; then, in the hour when the pressure has swung the hand past the danger marker and the red alert is about to sound, when the price of love has fallen so low that the market is closed for the day and there are only a few ancient sweepers, so tired they cannot stand, in the usually busy pits—then the quitting whistle sounds.

For a moment no one moves or breathes. It is a miracle—
that it happens every day does nothing to change it. Since
seven or eight or nine in the morning they have been waiting
for it; at eleven they dared not think; at two thirty they
despaired; since four they have been working in mechanical
fury, dreaming of hand-grenades and heads on poles, and
suddenly it is there, there, all over the shop, all over the city,
hanging from the corners of the buildings like a flag, the only
flag they have. It waves in the blue air of evening. This is the
third pattern, which is of release.

Strength comes back into the arms of the Empire State
Building. The knife is put back into the tool box to wait for
the day that cannot be borne, and suddenly the city is like a
great mother, calling her children home. Sealed in the roaring
tubes like current in a wire they flow under the iron carpet of
the city. The tunnels, like mouths of great fish, spew out the
wandering Jonahs; the doors of banks like mausoleums, the
hole-in-the-wall shops like installment-plan graveyards, give
up their corpses, and all over the city the crippled sheriffs with
glass keys at their belts open the stocks in which thousands
have been locked.

It is the hour and the pattern of renewal and release.

And after the last cup of coffee, after the baseball scores
and the news report, when honor itself is lost, before it is
necessary to think of sleep and of waking and of the new day
which will be just like the one that has died, there is the
pattern of search, when it only seems necessary to say the
right word, to find the right bar, the right girl, the right
memory, when it seems not only necessary but easy: to find
the street where the way was lost, when the hand was shaken
that can never be shaken again and you went away and left
yourself there, the only part that could be of use to you now.

This is the pattern of search.

It always ends in a bar or a fight, or sorrow, or sex. It always ends in sleep and never quite there, for there are always the long dead empty streets in the moonlight, corners to be turned; you are a piece on an enormous chess board and it is up to you to move.

But you do not have to move, because you are the neutral man. You can wait. The streets run up and down and cross each other. The squares are red or black. Nevertheless there are only so many pieces on the board. There are only so many moves that are open to each one. There are limits to possibilities and no matter how hard one thinks, there are certain things which cannot be done. This is the comfort of the neutral man in the pattern of search.

III Night

You prepare yourself for the pragmatical circus.

In the morning, despair; in the evening, hysteria; and in between, the patterns of alienation. In the mechanics of morning they are fastened screaming to the endless belt of necessity; in the day, in the patterns of profit and loss, they are moved on the board in a plan they cannot foresee, but evening hangs on the wind a flight of grand pianos and the blue key of hope which is meant to fit all doors. These are the masks of the day: the hunted, the victim, the hunter. These are the desires of the day: to be free, to destroy, to escape. The domain of the alarm clock, the domain of indifferent bells, the domain of the neon. Morning, noon and evening.

In the evening, when the first stars calm the disordered sea, and the lights, soft on the streets, run like a school of fish, when the bars like confessionals, when the theaters like magic rites, call to renewal, and the little winds of personal hope cool the prairies of wild flesh, then the avenue opens, the houses move apart, and there seems no limit on the private wish.

The domain of neon is the color of desire. The papers have all been read. History sleeps for the night. Behind the barred windows, in the tastefully decorated padded cell, the restless lunatic has stopped screaming, and the last suicide of the day, wearily climbing the stairs of the ninety-fourth floor, pauses at the landing in a moment of release and begins the long descent into another dream.

Begins the pragmatical circus, the carnival of pursuit. At Times Square they are unlocking the cages, but already the desperate early ones have crawled into the lions' den and the snake pit, spreading the elastic bars. The unlucky ones shake hands with the slot machines, and the loveless sit in the booths taking an endless picture of themselves. Some with champagne, some with a can of smoke, investigate the pressures on the floor of the alcohol sea, but all these are the Old China Hands in the spreading Asia of a lost continent. They have been there before, and they will return again, because they have international passports fashioned of stainless steel and lettered in Esperanto. Their pockets are full of slugs to fit turnstiles not yet invented; they were born with the necessary maps outlined on the palms of their hands. But there are others.

On the Great Plains of Childhood, a couple are approaching the Great Divide at the speed of fumbling hands. Their only protection is ignorance, a .22 mounted on a .45 frame, and for provisions they have a half pint of cheap whiskey. They are coming down the old Chisholm Trail in a secondhand Ford. They lie under the black cliffs, clothed only with each other. Beyond them the last of the buffalo graze, humped, snorting and doomed to perish, but these two do not notice, lying in rapt marmorean ease. These are the pioneers. In these, perhaps, is the necessary redemption, for they too are birds of the evening, passing a savage coast, and are not part of the circus. But to you, the neutral man, it appears only that they have not yet been captured, that the grand piano has not yet been mechanized. How long will the warmth last in the cold winter? When the windows are broken in the cyclonic vacuum of despair and the cold winds come into bed smelling of the dead buffalo and the vanished tribes, smelling of the timeclock and the morning whistle, how long shall that honey breath hold out? You do not consider these things, for it is the role of the neutral man to be an eye among the blind; you observe only that the circus moves into the streets.

On the atolls of parks are the hunted lovers, with all around the shark-toothed roaring waters of Manhattan. Their clothes are out of style and moonlight like acid falls through their torn hats. The coral cuts their feet, they have no guns or fishlines, the monsoon season is at hand, there is a blight on the coconut trees, and they are outside the shipping lanes in a latitude that has not yet been computed. These are the survivors.

The waters of hysteria move up the human markers. At eleven o'clock hope begins to be abandoned. Everything is tried to see if it will work. The opposite of the noonday plan is the midnight dream and the nexus is irony, but the opposite of the pragmatical hunt is accident and the nexus is chance, and though the beggar fall into the bed of the banker's wife, it is only when he has become impotent from hunger. The express starts for Buzzard's Bay, jumps the rails and pulls into the station at Tallahassee; but the dispatcher had written Omaha, and the engineer had wanted to go to Duluth. Red into black, odd to even.

The mechanical piano gets stuck on the one tune that should be forgotten and neighs brass notes like a randy stallion. The bells have broken loose and float above the city ringing all the hours at once, and if the arsonist manages to burn down the fire station, it is only because that night there will be no other fires. In the police stations they are beating a murderer. He has confessed and is telling the truth but the police cannot believe him until they have beaten him into recanting. The fixed dice forget their cunning and the street signs their numbers.

Still, no one can surrender. There is still the last bar to be tried; there is the possibility of finding the whore that will satisfy, the drink that will quench, the hope that will survive the night and lift its sunflower face in the morning to color the world with a different light.

Nightmare city, where the lost tribes are hunting the hairy mammoth. Cracks open in the pavements. Walls collapse. Hell is around every corner and the devil under every bed, the usual hell, the familiar devil, there is nothing even terrifying about him, and there is just the chance that he may, at last, turn out to be the one friend that has always been needed, as long acquaintance sometimes changes to love. But there will always be morning, morning, and as the clock hand moves toward twelve, toward the hour of sleep and of transformations, the dark shadow of morning falls on the white night. They are slowly sheathed in that lead against the chance X-rays of hope. That sunflower seed will never be planted.

And the streets slowly begin to empty as the vitality is dissipated. The liquor in the bottles undergoes a chemical change until alcohol is as weak as blood. Coming on each other suddenly, the old friends shake hands, but the hands come loose at the ends of the sleeves and they are forced to stuff them awkwardly into their pockets. One meets the necessary woman at the edge of the park, but she is sleep-walking, and he finds suddenly that he has forgotten his own tongue and can speak only a language which he cannot understand. Another finds a body dead in a gutter but when he calls the police it is himself that the wagon takes away to the morgue. Accidental death.

All the chances are taken, all the riders are down. The grand pianos are there, but they have been mechanized. The blue key works, but it opens the wrong doors.

Living and Dying 5

Uses of the Lost Poets

for Don Gordon

The poems of others he clipped and saved in those distant summers—
No farther from him than himself—have faded into the dark,
Almost . . . the dew that died on the dry page weathering away—
Out of its image—to climb the ladder of sun and wind
To the cradling sea gathered; and the metaphorical diamond,
That once worked names on glass, gone back to the soft country
Of carbon, memory, letters . . .

                          to the wounds of the bituminous man.

Child of fancy, what did you hope from those distant voices
Crying immortal anguish in the fallen world of your desk
Abandoned, now? Oh, the boy was only trying
To climb on the dewy stairs of the poem his contemporary built
Toward the sound of a friend, perhaps, or the name cut into glass, some
Thing to hold more permanent than a flower pressed in a book—
If the firefly is summer, the poem *might* be the star of time.

A century of cicadas has burnt holes in those paper heavens
In the few breaths that he drew while the poems lay curled in sleep
In his grave notebook saved—gone into time like smoke
With the winking generations of the firefly, the dew, the impermanent
Diamond . . .

              And how he must fly his own kite in the dark of the moon
To gather what lightning may lead him dangerously out of that dark
And up the homing stairway to set a light on his desk.

For he is no boy, now, but himself the bituminous man:
Burning: and not to be diamond but for usefulness of that light—
His own—for others: the wink and bite of international
Code to guide or home on for those on blind ways: to save
(Now that stars fall, the zodiac shifts and the lodestar drifts and lies)
Or hope to save (from loss and terror of these times)
To save the lonesome traveller lost on the nightbound roads.

No Caribbean Cruise

for Meridel LeSueur

Like Rome or Pah-Gotzin-Kay,
The Revolution is a *place*.

Because of the shortage of maps,
Few can find it.

But there are real trees there . . .
And: children.

The water is pure
But too cold for tourists to drink.

Totems (I)

In the fall
Feathers appear in the tassels
On Robert Bly's serape.

Without his knowledge or consent
His feet start a heavy dance
Like the dance of a prairie chicken.
All at once he is spinning
Like the reel of an old fanning mill,
Glowing in many colors as his phases change.

Lifting light as a top
He lofts up onto a fence post
The soles of his shoes smoking
In a smell of burning cedar.

Slowly geese appear in the sky.
He leaps up to join them,
Laughing and honking south.

Totems (II)

A slow and heavy work horse—
A Clydesdale or Percheron—
Like a fenced-in cloud
Moves in the little pasture
Aimlessly. It is Jim Wright.

He moves delicately, avoiding
The round puffs of the clover
With his huge hooves. His fetlocks
Are hairy and melancholy.

Toward evening he goes
To the old watering trough.
He stands looking at the mossy stones on the bottom.
After a while he remembers
To lower his head and drink.

Totems (III)

If you follow his tracks in the deep snow you can't believe it—
Sometimes a two-legged, sometimes a four-legged, sometimes a winged,
                                                                sometimes
A boat—or a barn door—it's certainly Merwin!

After a while you notice the tracks going off in several directions
                                                    at once.
Then a hand flies past, calling out in many tongues!
It is the left hand—the other has gone on ahead
Looking for wood and water . . .

When the parts of the body have all disappeared,
We hear the voice speaking from the edge of darkness . . .
The voice speaking out of the ground
Out of the air
Speaking inside our heads . . .

Totems (IV)

Here is a huge boulder wandered down from the mountains . . .
It is the kind of rock that hates gravity, has a difficult time
Falling and has had to come roundabout
                                         slowly
                                              following
The rivers—
          stopping
                  often—
                          to grow moss on its rough knees
Before reaching the Kapowsin Tavern . . .
                                        a long time travelling
And a lot of time standing around in the dark, alone, almost silent.

This hugy rip-water rock can only be Richard Hugo
With his shoes full of salmon!
                              Quiet as a fishing bear
He waits under the green gloom of the rainy trees
For days
        listening
                to something far off
                                    above
Timberline.
          Meanwhile the fish are climbing over his feet.
At highwater time we hear him: singing a loud cold song.

Totems (V)

It is the special kind of night that Alvaro likes. It's not—
Or not merely—the full moon in this water-spill somewhere
In Venice L.A. It's a—kind of—let's call it a configuration:
Moon.
       Water.
          Night.
               The deep heart of the singer:
A guitar has sunk in 6 fathoms of honey . . .
                       And remember:
The secret oils of Venice have transformed the transforming moon . . .

. . . .

Anyway: the moon in the water. And this lunatic frog—
It *can't* be anyone but Alvaro Cardona-Hine at his old stunt:
Singing.
       He would like to have the moon, perhaps, the scabrous
Changing filth and flirt of the air-less black acres of
Night space, as prisoner here in these back and blasted lots . . .
And he sings.
       The moss grows over him.
               He does not care.
                     It is his
Art.
       Hu-m-m-m-m-m-m-m
               hu-m-m-m-m-m
                   hu-m-m-m-m-m

. . . .

Nor does the moon care, falling into the west
Like a drunken mother into an oven, her face beginning to
Char in the changing light—and all the oils and acids of
Sinister Venice cannot preserve her.

It is then that Alvaro
Changes into a fox-squirrel and leaps to the limb of a tree!
The moon is a floating nut, the last one he needs for winter,
And he begins to coax it home in his soothing voice—
With an occasional bark to let it be known who's boss.
This stimulates blasphemy and early TV among the more human
Neighbors.
             After what seems like a long time, if you are a
Squirrel-singer, the moonnut dissolves in the acid pool
Or sinks to the bottom.
                    Dawn, like a drunken ship, staggers
Into port at San Pedro, hearse-horn-mourning for all of us dead at sea.

                    . . . .

It has been a prosperous night for our poet.
                              He stuffs the fox gear
Into the back of a station wagon near Shotwell's greenhouse.
Then, forgetting they are aerodynamic anomalies that cannot fly,
(And that *he* cannot fly) he changes into a bumblebee. He has remembered
Where, past a cut in the hills, lies a solid mile of clover.
He cannot wait for a moment—there is always too much to be done.
Humming a little—tuning the void—he is on his way
To serenade a 90 acre field of disordered and premature honey.
It will keep him busy a while: sounding many disguises . . .

There will always be time for the necessary transformations.

Totems (VI)

Somewhere a knife is sleeping in its own shadow—
And so the shadow of the knife is sharper than the knife itself,
Since the Shadow never sleeps; or sleeps and feeds at once—
Both at home on the third rail somewhere toward Brooklyn.

There are no surprises here in the green shadow of money
As sour as shchi. But there are eyes everywhere, larger
Than clocks in subways or clocks in police substations where time is—
How can be? Where time's night always? Yet is—yet time is—money.

Certainly some of these clocks are the eyes of a night heron—
Or David Ignatow! Telling and reading the times by foxfire
By fictions and fractions of many-foiled failing and falling so-busy
Bodies—O Jesus the money-felled swampsky greengrosses their light!

For the night heron, fishing in his dark waters, the lights
Of these falling dogstars and starlets are the fire sales of the spirit.
These shades are so fit and full (sometimes) they fatten that shadow
Where the knife sharpens its teeth feeding on misery and hate.

It is here in this shadow the night-heron David keeps heart's-eye open.
His head turns; clockwise; he is wise in the ways of subways:
(Where the angry ghost-fish slide or glide in the shapes of their hungers)
These nightrivers underground may lead to death . . . or home.

Still it is hard to stand in the swamplight of failing systems—
And on one leg to boot!—counting the dead and seeking
(All ways) the shape of the human. We must let him go
(Sometimes) (friends) (alone) to look at (perhaps) the moon.

Revolutionary Frescoes—the Ascension
in memory of Walter Lowenfels

On that morning when the Unknown Revolutionary rises
From his bed in the Veterans' Hospital in Fargo, North Dakota,
There will be free cigarettes for everyone and no lumps in the porridge!
Trumpets will sound and resound from the four corners of the world!
The four blue-blowers and commissars of the vagrant and workless winds,
Standing at the round earth's blazing corners, in arms,
Will organize the demonstration: Marx, Engels, Lenin,
Che—the last and youngest at the western corner with machine gun.

Then, in the hospital corridors the walking wounded will fly
As a Blakean column of pure spirit toward the operating room
And the rotting flesh, bed-bound will rise up in song!
The walking delegates with wooden legs will race through the halls
And the wheel-chairs, now winged—the wheels within wheels of Fellow-worker
    Ezekial—
Will sport it in the very whiskers of Marx as he beams from his plinth
Near the ceiling of the north corner! And all four commissars will sound
The timbrel and the fraternal harp and the mouth organ and the guitar,
And the heavenly host will chant, led by Woody and Cisco:
Everything or Nothing, Comrades! All of us or none!

Then the rolling tomb will arrive blazing with slogans and flowers!
But *no gardenias*, dear Comrades! Damn all bourgeois conventions!
Let us have something simpler instead. Geraniums, maybe—
From the window-boxes of the poor. And, from the woods, red cardinals—and trillium!
To stand for the flowering unity of theory and practice and daring—
But leave it to the Mexican and Italian sections to organize: they *know*!
Finally the heavenly cadres have all in hand—no more
To do but fly up in a great hosting of real and hallucinatory
Light!
        They fly up . . .
                Farewell, Comrade!
                        You did your share.

And now, in the pause that follows, I remember walking with you
And your other comrade, Walt Whitman, beside the Jersey shore
While he talked of news of these states and the foiled revolutionaires
Out of an earlier time; and we run to keep up with his stride.
Himself with his beard full of butterflies, you with the moon on your forehead!
Midnight ramblers and railers! By the cradle, endlessly rocking,
Of a fouled contaminant sea you both saw clean and young . . .
Father of the dream, you said he was; father of poets.
I see you now in the Shades, old Double Walt, dear outlaws.

And now we must straighten the chairs in the meeting room.
A few need dues-stamps to fill out their Party Books.
A few buy the works of the Lost Poet at the Literature table—
A bit dubious for all that the young Lit-comrade says.
Finally we divide the left-over cigarettes,
Cutting some in half so that everything comes out even.
All squared away. All in good proletarian order,
We leave the place ship-shape for the next delegation to use—
Though such uprisings don't happen every day . . .

News Of Your Death

For Mac Blair

First, a stunning numbness:
Like touching a live wire . . .
Or the shock of reality entering through my broken arm
When I fell from a horse . . .
The smell of the snake just before the rattle . . .

Then: the feeling the fish has
The instant the dynamite explodes
Just under the thick ice.

Soapbox Speech for Kennedy

Salute!
       —that hero, who, without counting
The downcast light in the eyes of the newfallen dead
Gathered his valor;
Who, without blood on the shining edge of his word,
Prevailed;
Who, without armor, achieved;
Who, with his love carried the town and the day—
Praise him!

                    . . . .

I am not talking, friends, about happy Jack Kennedy
The bodacious baby bronc-buster from the bonny braes of old Back Bay
Shouting *Powder River let 'er buck!* to the well-heeled merry-go-round mounts
                                of hard money:
Those rocking-horse herds of many mortgages charging
Across the guilt-edged prairie-dogged lawns of his father's first million.

I am not talking, comrades, good buddies, about the catholic candor of that
                            prince of purpose,
That Darius Green of demo-demagoguery stunting at an altitude of six feet two
Over, above and around and through the flat preachments and hairy prophecy
Of political platforms heel-high to heels—unslateable scripts
Full of migrating periods pricked out in the universal language of the dead.

No, I am not speaking, friends, comrades, non-voting
Cats, compañeros, of *that* particular Kennedy. Haven't I been there—
Canoe of dialectic shooting the rapids of his careful laughter;
Don't I know—and I'm telling you now, fellow-workers:
There was instant Ivy sprung from the Old Oaken Head of Eisenhower agog in all
                            winds.

Well—the tic-tac-toe of class consciousness is faster than Univac:
There's no harp in that Harp's house and no salt in his dolor!
Scissorbill, meat-head Reagan-head HARK!
Plutonian diseases of the mineral world
Rust the green monies of that springtime king!

. . . .

No, lads, sweet ladies, I'm talking about *Sam* Kennedy—
Size Aleph Three halo—man too big to fit in—
To fit in his own novels. —hey there old moonfitter! I see you,
Great Cock of Light on the swinging vane of your petrified song
Blasting the wizened sun from the black entrapments of the dollar-circled sea!

What fever of unloosed light did you bring to the fifty-star dark
Of these benighted States! What diamond ponies of radiant love
Stampeding out of the badlands of a glass guitar!
And against the statutes of popcorn and the protocols of chrome
Eagles of smoke and whisky at your right and left hands fly!

Alas, what colors have bled from our private flags since you went
Single-footing down the blazed trail of cold lang sign
Toward the Bad Lands. . . . Bituminous anguish in the early snow . . .
The Bomb sings in the Counting House . . . the Companions discuss
The merits of the demirep Agony Man of the double-headed Party of Death.

It's a long time you been gone old man a long time.
I remember you, helmsman, at the prow of your chisel, discovering
The soft things that shelter in stone I remember your luminous journeys
Into the night of mahogony. I remember the working class heroes
Which your prying and rebel eye lead forth from the prison tree.

Times change. Fellow-workers, this sculptor and singer once
Built him a harpsichord for love of the music in it.
Let the President, fellow-workers, build him a voting machine
For the love of the abstract polis. And let us, fellow-workers,
Cast up our ballot. For my dead man alive, or that president of the dead.

Echoes inside the Labyrinth 6

"Christmas Section III continues *Part Three* of Thomas McGrath's on-going long narrative poem *Letter To An Imaginary Friend*. *Part One* begins with early childhood on a North Dakota farm, goes on to early work experiences, sex, college, political awakenings, World War II, and beyond. *Part Two* picks up the themes of *Part One* and re-sees them in the light of new circumstances, and "is concerned with the offering of evidences for a revolutionary miracle and with elaborating a ceremony out of these materials to bring such a miracle to pass."

The whole of "Christmas Section" (*Part Three* of *Letter to an Imaginery Friend*) concerns going to and coming from midnight Mass on Christmas Eve and what happens in between—as seen by a young boy in the 1920s, and remembered and told by someone much older. The narrative voice changes back and forth between them. "Section III" (printed here) begins with the young boy's family arriving at his grandparents' home. In #1-4 of this section the boy treks to church to make his confession, returns to grandfather's barn where the men are passing a bottle of moonshine and swapping stories, and completes a mission to invite his father's irreverent friend, Cal, and "his girl" over to celebrate Christmas after the family returns from Mass. #5 is the Mass.

Letter to an Imaginary Friend, Part One and Two is available in a single volume from Swallow Press/Ohio University Press. Sections I and II of Part Three are available in Thomas McGrath's *Passages Toward the Dark*, Copper Canyon Press.

Christmas Section III

from Letter to an Imaginary Friend

1

And under those bell-shaped shadows from the continent of iron, we come
To my grandparents' home.

                  It sits on the edge of town:

                                          one foot
Out on the Old-Prairie pasture, the other under the street lamps,
Midpoint between poverty and the police.

                                 The house is transported
Halfway to heaven by the sacred season, by the gallimaufry
Of uncles, aunts, cousins, friends and simple nightstrollers
Gathered, and now tiptoe at the tops of their voices shouting—
(Out of imperfect confusion to argue a purer chaos)—
Except for the wee ones, already, six to a bed, sleeping.
Blameless, too young for big-game sin, which begins at seven,
They sleep in heavenly peace, their manifest souls glowing
Faintly as they hover over those dreaming heads in the gloom
Of the chill outlying upstairs bedrooms

                               insulated
From the downstairs talk and laughter and bright dominion of sin:
That brief kingdom of sensuous flesh for this moment protected
From the fear of the dooms and demons in the downcellar dark, waiting.
And while they wait their turns to make their midnight confessions
I run through the winter-chilled streets to lay out my summer sins.

2

A sugar snow, like powdered marble, under the steepling
Light of the high moon climbs to where the Cross
Lifts itself toward heaven above the now-sleeping bell.
Mast without sails! The church is a timeless transport: yawl,
Schooner or cat-boat: cut-down descendant of the tall ships
The cathedrals once were—dreadnaughts a thousand feet high and long
As all the centuries . . .

            cargo of souls, soonering . . .
                                  ship of the dead.

Could not have been Christ did this: sent up cathedrals like missiles—
The hard rock-candy mountain of Notre Dame,
                                the seven-
Layer cake at Pisa or Sienna's maple sugar.
This is the Father's doing—the Father's and Humankind's—
Man will do anything to be saved but save himself . . .

—But here's no cathedral nor all-topsails-set spiritual frigate!
More like a barge or scow tied up for the night, our church
Is pegged to a scrawny pine tree where a stray dog howls and pisses,
Now, as I enter the arena at the edge of the stained glass
For my sinfishing at the troubled headwaters of my little soul.

The colored glass of the windows leads me to leaden roads
Through greeny pastures where the young lamb skips . . .
There the shepherd's crook ne'er turned a hair or horn
And all's Adam-and-Eden in the Eve-less morning, sinless:
A summery pastorale . . .
                   false as the rosy glass.
That fire that cannot singe a sleeve has burnt millions
And not in hell but closer to home—(Let there be light,
O Napalm!)—
            The leads and leads of the windows take me
Past these false fields to the pride of the donors names:
To Mr. & Mrs. P. J. Porkchop and all the rest
Of the local banditti and bankers, the owners of God;
                            to Presidents
Elect, of Rotaries;
                  to Judges; and sheriffs: high and low—
Lifetakers and deathmakers and justicefakers all—
And all the family off-brands, culls, gulls, lames and lowgrades
(But pukka sahibs, sirdars, eponymous bwanas of the Celestial Raj
Nathless) . . .
             united in unholy marriage of Money and Law.

And the First Law is: there shall *be* but One Law
To read: "This Law is only for those who can afford it."
"They have sold the righteous for silver and the needy for a pair of shoes,"
Saith the poet (Amos), *"who make the ephaw small and the shekel great."*
The MoneyTree stands at the center of this primeinterest Eden
Above the donors' names.
                              "'n' how d'ya like *them* apples?"
Asks Bill Dee—or *Yasna* 30, the *Gathas*.
Where the Worm gnaws at the roots of Yggdrasil—where *here* is
Room for the Li'l Pickaninny, him b'long God?

I enter the church. And there, past the Holy-Water-dowsers
Is my Latter-Day Kulak, George P., doing a penance:
Down on his skinny shin-bones lofting up lauds to His Lord!

The church is dusky and cold like the twilight of early morning.
But the dusk is lit by the flash in Father Mulcahy's face:
Ah—that bullion-buck-toothed and gold-arpeggioed glare—
Dental ivory as of elephant boneyards and lost Yukon
Cheechako's tenstrikes: the bright bonanza of an upstanding gravestone grin!
In that sharksflare of facial lightning he mistakes for a smile,
He takes his fatherly leave of a woman ninety years old,
And gets back to the central business of sinbusting. I'm the next case.

In the confessional, kneeling, I feel my bonds with that world
I am too young to enter now—kingdom of flesh and the devil—
But I sense all around me, like a prisoner brought to a midnight cell,
The names, the outrages, and the invitations spelled on the walls.
From the body of the church comes a scatter of prayer from an earlier penance.
The confessional falls in its shaft toward the great sin-mine below.

But I cannot see in *that* dark: my eyes are not
Opened: fully: (my puppy-dog eyes) to the rank and rare
Diamond and emerald gems that stud the sinfilled stopes
That lead toward the mother lode . . .

96

                                And yet it is sin I can smell
Around me now as the confessional rises again in its shaft:
The smell of hellfire and brimstone: spice and herb to that incense
Of sanctity and sweat: the stink of beasts and angels
                                                couplings . . .

And, in my child's heart, I do sense sin . . .
                                far off, maybe,
And grown-up and gowned in the glamour and grammar of loss
I cannot quite name (though I know all the names for sin, and its smell
And secret accent)—loss that begins somewhere beyond me—
Over the border from childhood, in that wild space where we
Turn into men and women in a gambler's dark where choice
Is reckless all ways.
                        Yes, I do know sin,
For haven't I felt the whole universe recoil at my touch?
And my mother weep for my damned ways?
                                        At my approach
The Sensitive Plant contracts its ten thousand feathery fingers
Into a green fist.
                        I have caused the sudden nova
Where the Jewel Weed's seed-box handgrenade explodes at my touch.
It is fear of my sin that changes the rabbit's color;
                                        my sin
That petrifies the wave into pelagic trance
Where the deep sea hides its treasures;
                                        it is from fear
Of me that the earthquake trembles in its cage of sleep and ennui;
From me the stars shudder and turn away, closing
Against my image the shining and million eyes of the night . . .

But the holy father is becoming incensed: against my shame
And my flaming peccadilloes he shakes down his theomometer
And thrusts it into my mouth to see how hot I burn,
What heights I can heat a hell to as spelled on a God-size scale—
"Get on with it boy," he says and I buckle down to my woes.

They hardly seem worth the Latin they were writ in nor the wrath that wrought
   them . . .
"Well?"
                Pride, Covetousness, Lust, Anger, Gluttony,
Envy and Sloth—the seven Capital and Capitalized sins—
They seem all beyond me.
                        "Speak up, boy! Speak up I say!"
"I was mean to many without meaning to be mean."
                              "Who were you mean to?"

"Everyone.
        Everything."
               "And that's all you can say for yourself?"
What could be worse?
               Impatience?
                 (He has it for both of us.)
                           "Have you ever
Taken the Lord's name in vain?"
               "Yes."
                   "How often?"
"Always."
        "Always?"
            "Always in vain I mean, Father.
It never helped."
         —"Ha-r-r-rumph!" (But uncertain.) "Get on!"

And I do get on . . .
             but all my sins seem so immensely tiny,
Not big enough to swear by: mere saplings of sins,
A pigwidgen patter, no more than jots and tittles
In the black almanac of adult industry: fingerling sins,
Cantlets and scantlings—gangrel and scallywag sins that will never
Come home to roost nor sing for their suppers: a parvitude of sins
All heading toward vanishing points like charmed quarks.

But out of these is a universe made. And my weak force
Essential . . .
                    —"Three Our Fathers and three Hail Marys," he says.
Small they might be but still of the essence . . .
                                        —and this is insult:
Our Fathers and Hail Marys—that is the penance
For children and old ladies! Surely I deserve better,
I at whom the distant galaxies flare and convulse, shuddering
At my indeterminant principle and sinister energy potential.

"Well, boy?"
                    "I think I deserve a harder penance, Father."
"Such as?"
                    "As among the Spiritual Works of Mercy, Father:
To instruct the ignorant. To admonish sinners."
                                        "It takes one to know one.
What else?"
                    "As among the Corporal Works of Mercy, Father:
To bury the dead. To visit those in prison."
                                        "All in time.
For now: three Our Fathers and three Hail Marys. Hop to it!"

It's less than I can face. "There's more, Father, there's more!"
"Then spit it out and get on with yez, y'little spalpeen!"

But what's the more to get on to? I call upon all the words
In the dictionary of damnation and not a damned one will come.
I pray for the gift of tongues and suddenly I am showered
With all the unknown words I have ever heard or read.

"I am guilty of chrestomathy, Father."
                                 He lets out a grunt in Gaelic,
Shifting out of the Latin to get a fresh purchase on sin.
"And?"
"Barratry,Father.
"And minerology . . .
"Agatism and summer elements . . .
"Scepticism about tooth fairies . . .
"Catachresis and pseudogogy . . .
"I have poisoned poissons in all the probable statistics . . .
"I have had my pidgin and eaten it too, Father . . .
"Put fresh dill on the pancakes . . .
"Hubris . . ."

(Get him on the ropes, groggy, still game, but wary.)
"Accidie . . .
"Mopery with intent to gawk . . .
"Anomy and mythophobia . . .
"Mañanismo . . .
"Jiggery-pokery and narcokleptomania . . .
"Animal husbandry . . .
"Nichivoism . . .
"Mooching and doddering . . .
"Florophilia and semantic waltzing . . .
"Dream-busting . . .
"Cthonic incursions on the mineral world . . .
"And all the Corconian debaucheries of my ancient P&Q-Celt forbears
And aftbears.
                 Father, I have eaten of the Forbidden
Fruit: dandelion greens—but refused cranberries with turkey."

A silence from beyond the border where the Latin begins. And then:
"You left out something."
                              "What's that, Father?"
                                             Anfractuosity."
                                                      "What's
That, Father?"
               "Three Our Fathers and three Hail Marys!"

Hell hath no fury like a sinner scorned.
                                  I try again:
"Zoomorphism."
             He's cautious. "Yes?"
                              "Father, I have failed
My grandfather's Animal Catechism, each inch and fur of the way!"
"And have ye now, my little parolee and logoklept?"
"Yea; though daily I do my self quiz in my Grandfather's terms and tones: VIZ:

    APED yr elders and bitters with Adder's tongue and the
      audacity of the Addax, jawboning like an Agamic Afghan
      Ass, multiplyin' and Alewivin' in Alligatorial Allegorial and
      editorial biases yr Antsy and granunclcy anymosities most monstress?
                              Aye! Aye! Oudad! Oudad!—I have!
                              And have you had
    BATs in yr belfry, Bees in yr bonnet, been Bird-brained
      and Beaver-struck? Badgered yr Da for dash or
      Saturday buckshee, tryin' to Bulldoze and daze
      the poor man till, totally Buffaloed, he turns loose
      of the totemic nickel so you may monarchize an ice-cream
      cone or play the weekendin' social Butterfly,
      O me bucko?
                              —I have

                                                          And have you not
CATercorned on the strayed and error, gone kittywampus
        through a one-way woods, soundin' yr Capercailie,
        horse as an Irish bull among the small concealed
        circular saws of Cicadas buildin' a wild roof on
        the afternoon? Did you Cow the Chipmunks then?
        In all Condor, have you not sunk to the heights
        of desirin' to do a bit of Coyote on the benign
        burgers of this part of the continental
        bench?
                                        —I have!
DOGged it have you not sometimes—while Doggedly
        persistin' in the errors of yr wise? And deep-divin'
        into yr pride divined yrself the lost Dolphin
        of pelagic palatinates, their depth-soundin'
        economies dumbfoundered on the tides of sweat
        from drowned sailors—and ye never guessed why the sea
        was salt?
                                        —I have!
                                                          And have you not
FOXed yr small clothes dirty as a dudeen, Ferretin' about in
        dromedary domains the desert fathers would fain drop dead in,
        and all for the Turkish Delight of some whoreson cameldung
        heathen sultanic satanic solecism or Islamic oral doodad?
        And yrself—to jump from the desert to the sea—yrself
        a mere puddler in those deep waters, a small Fry among
        leviathans and lower than a Floundered Fluke?
                                        —I have! I am! I have!
GROUSEd in the house as a layabout, have'nt ye, Gullin' yr poor parents
        with the etiological biography of imaginary terminal migraines
        while those poor Grunts yr brothers and fellow-workers sowed
        their sweat in the fields?
                                        —I have! I have!

HAREd about, haven't ye, hedgin' and Hedgehoggin' to yrself
    the Hog's share of that communal leisure earned by yr fellows doin'
    time at hard labor, arrogantly arrogatin' and unduly expropriatin'
    forty acres for yourself out of the social collective of the
    People's Clock? And it the south forty at that—for shame, for shame!
                                    —*I have! I have! I have!*
IRISH SETTEEd, didn't you, dogsbody, prolongin' the noonday
    dispensation from labor with all the pious presumption
    of a runaway Avignon Pope? Io moth Impaladed on a horn of the midday light!
                                    —*I did! I was! I am!*
JACKASSed around for donkey's years didn't you—connin' the
    distaff side for the makin's of a many-colored
    coat while yr brothers sweated in Egyptian slavery? And
    not too young to woof at the warp of an innocent spinnin' Jenny?
                                    —*I'm not! I did! I'm not!*"
                    ****

"Let's get back to the *I's*, where I feel ye're more at home."
"Yes, Father," I say, irising out Grandfather's oneiric fancies.
"That's an alphabet could be sold in the fur trade!"
He says.
            Further, I think, Father; or farther than sin.
"Ye're livin' aloft, my son—yer 'I' 's high as the mountains of Mourne.
But we'll all come down as low as the Red River River Valley
In time."
            (As the Worm gnaws at the roots of Yggdrasil—
In time.)
        Aye.
            "Father?
                    —Gimme my penance, Father."
"Three Our Fathers and three Hail Mary's—and get ye gone!"

And I'm out on the street—*should* have been: all the Stations of the Cross—
Cut your own timber and bring your own hammer and nails!
But I bow to my piddling penance. Then, in the darkly shining,
In the bell-surrounded night I run for my Grandfather's barn.

I remember it from Sunday visits in the long days of the summer:
The rafters furry with moss and the brightmetal harness bosses
Blurred with rust from the lack of use—Grandfather, retired,
Retired his team to the pasture except for sacred occasions.
Now, in lantern shine—color of straw and September—
The rafters drip with the white milk of the frost.

                                             The men
Sit in an empty stall on whiskery bales of hay.
They spit and smoke.
                       A bottle of moonshine roves, slowly,
From hand to hand, the circle. They'll still be "fasting from midnight"
When they go to sup on the bread and wine of this night's communion.

It is the hour when the animals knelt and the Wise Men came.
We're all in waiting but no one awaits.
                                 In the Hour of the Beasts
No knee knelt never.
                  Out of the dark
Of a far stall a stallion farts and stales.
A rainy sound of pee—summery—and geldings snort and stomp
And a mare whinnys—but the stud's too old to remember.

The men are swapping Ralph Wristfed stories: *Rolf Ristvedt*
To give him his proper name—the archetypal Norwegian.
Bob Edwards is there—who, on the high steel,
Walked through the wintry skies of cities; and Dale Jacobson,
The tormented one; and Robert Bly of the Mistly Isles.
And Martinson, David, and Mark Vinz and Sam Hamill,
Bert Meyers, Charlie Humbolt and David Cumberland-Johnson,
And Fred Whitehead and Richard Nichson with his gambler's smile.
Also Don Gordon, who'd left his mountainy perch

To join us in the mysteries of the joyous season; and Hart Crane
Who would later study the undersea life in deeps far
Far deeper, more fearsome, than those of the Mexican Gulf.
And there was our neighbor, Brecht, who sang both high and low
And mostly in German; and a small man who looked like a turtle and came from Chile.
Poets all of them. And my father, that quiet man, chief among chiefs—
Seemed so to me in those green years: and now as I say it.

And Edwards is telling:
                    how Questers three (for three
And thrice times three) long years and far had ranged
This fallen world.
                    Reedy registers and Pardoners once—
But now Knights greatly errant were; and bound in skins
Three several colors: hued by different suns.
White, black and brown-yellow, faced they th' indigenous blasts
Of distant lands and lorn; dreck dared they: dunged
Oft by shit-slinging multi-mitted mobs; and manful their doom, though sore!
These three yclept Tom, Dick and Harry were: men most admired!
More than admired: for that they kept the Quest
By ragged margints, tatterdemalion,
Of ragamuffin worlds whose ends alway and once and now,
Both woof and warp, fray out into the maternal dark.
And in this seach much maladventure was,
And much the matter of it, sung both high and low,
If teller telleth true. "'Struth!" cries the fabulist bard!

What sought they then these Questers Three? God-bitten, they
Searched for word of the Risen One: He who in myth
Is robed: He whom the prophets, age after bloody age,
Forecast in vain.
              The Son of God some say his holy name
Is. Or Wakan Tanka, others; Or Papa Legba—
Many and strange His names from Christ to Quetzalcoatl!
And now the False Ones come, in every age and nation,
Proclaimed The Chosen One.
                 Prophecy to doctrine to dogma—
All is decline: while stained-glass windows rise: by hierarchies,
Fraudulent all, conjured: by fakir and hoodoo man,
By mullah and iman, bonze, houngan and Holy Daddy.
"Oh! Pestilential priestcrafts!" cry they three!
But do not falter in their desperate quest.
                   To oracles far
As the world's navel they go as pilgrims. Wisemen and fools
They suffer the foolish wisdom of.
                 To midnight magic
At last they turn: to horiolation and mystic mantology,
To horuspication, sortilege, sibylline prognostations,
To casting the bones of sheep and translating entrails of horses,
Divining by tea leaves, by shadows, by dough, by salt, by water,
By the amount of rust on the bodies of cars, by the guts of clocks—
Astromancy, bibliomancy, cretinomany
Dactyliomancy, estispicy, gerontomancy—
And so, by such foul practice, falling at last so low
They must stick beans in their noses to ken the shape of the wind.

At length, by slow devise, wend they their wary way
To precinct sacred where sage Ralph Wristfed dwells.
There, in the Lutheran light, Norwegian, of nameless stars,
(Where June is a winter month) the Big Augur (or Ogre
For so some scholars read the heiratic epithet)
Broadcasts his wisdom to the random winds.
                                        A far country, that one,
And ruled by the Triple Goddess, whose three thrice-sacred names
Are Uff-da, Ish-da and Who-da—reading from left to right.
And there they three the fateful question ask (saith Edwards, Bard)
Of Wristfed (Venered) re: the Slain and Risen God.

Good answer gives he them of Him of Whom they him
Ask: viz: Whose *Who's* He Whom they Him (for them) do beg
Some nonprominal words to parse their way through the woods.
"—Whose *Who's* is He?" (cries Bardic Bob in ombred umbrage);
"Well might they ask Ralph Wristfed Who *He* was!"

And Wristfed, levin-leaper, with more sentence than syntax,
(O hyperpronomical priest!) lays out the story plain:
How man killed God;
                    how the dead God, in a cave,
                                            was walled;
(Ah, stony limits!)
                    but how, on that third day, at dawn,
Lo! He riseth! He shineth! The heavens are rolled asunder!

"We see the Light!" the Questors cry.
                            But Wristfed, loath
Too much to cheer them, says: "It is the light He fears:
For if His shadow Self He sees, He goes back in . . ."
"Back in the cave!" they cry. "And then?"
                            Quoth Wristfed: "Then . . .
Then—well, it's six weeks more hard winter, Gentlemen!"

****

They laugh, in sorrow; sorrow in their laugh.
                                        "Oh, Christ!
Poor bloody groundhog!" someone says.
                                        Then: silence.

Christcrossed between Christmas and Easter, between this Now and that *Never*
(Between Lisbon and Lisbon, Nothing and Revolution)
Between birth always-and-everywhere and their Never-and-Nowhere—
(Unless Nowhere is *Now here* of the Resurrection)
They wait.
                And are waiting still.
                                As I write this
                                                still
In that
        silence

                                4

                        And I, on my father's business again,
Go out into the cold night (where the joyous houses
Are still drifting between earth and heaven, levitating
Or hung on lunar chains from the rim of a wan moon
That is half devoured now by a shift of cloud)
                                —go,
As my father bids me, to find his friend, the man I know as Cal,
(Who is wintering over with us in one of the hard years)
And ask if he wants to ride out after mass and have Christmas with us.
"He's got this girl," my father says. (And we both nod).
"He may want to stay with her, you see. No, you don't, I guess . . .
But . . ." I nod and he smiles. "And as for goin' to mass, well he . . .
Would avoid it like the devil shuns holy water," we say in chorus.
"Ah, but there's faster ways to heaven than walkin' on your knees, my son!
(But don't tell your mother I said it!) And Cal's a good man, the best."

Maybe he is; but I don't know that, yet.
                            I'm still
Green ("in the savannas of my years, the blithe and fooling times")
Before my baptism in the fields of work and want and class war,
Before Cal was confirmed my brother, teacher and comrade
In the round dance and struggle that continues as long as we do.

                    ****

On a mission of armed revolutionary memory!
                            (But I don't know that yet.)
I go my little way through the ice-black streets,
Empty, of the dreaming and joyful town.
                            A cranky and fitfull wind,
Backing and filling, lifts a scrim of scene-shifting snow
And the streets disappear, reappear, open and close like a maze.
But I know these labyrinthine ways and steer by the stars,
Or like a dog-barking navigator, hugging the coast,
I take my bearings by sound, hearing the Burnses' cow
Unspool the cud of her Christmas silence with a long moo,
Or a musical bar of indignant song, a night-blooming rooster
Cock-alarming the town from down on its southern shore.

I came to the house through the back yard, past rosebower and byre
Where something breathing, and probably brown, snorts and shifts,
Rubbing the barnwall interior dark. (It was not, I think,
Not the Mithraic bull, though his time is Christmas too.)
At the backdoor steps, old toothless terror, a dog's on guard,
Chained to the property he's too worn out to protect—
Poor beast all hide and howl, but he summons Cal to the door.

The house is that of a retired banker—doubly retired
In the season when money retires to the shores of its tropical south.
Only the help is at home—the maid: Cal's girl, who holds
The keys to this mouldering Plutonic mansion. When Master's away
The maid will play! (And the Wandering Man will have his day!)
She has the key to the house and they both have keys to each other—
I sense this, seeing their faces (cut-outs against the light
Where the banker's birch logs flare in the open fireplace flue)—
Faces flushed with a secret content I'm too young to desire,
And a little, maybe, with drink from the Mason jar of moon.

"And so," says Cal, "it's the birthday of poor old Jerusalem Slim,
The Galillean gandy-dancer and Olympic water-walkin' champ!
And the pious are slappin' their chests and singin' their *You-Betcha's* and *I-Gotcha's*—
All peace on earth for about five seconds. But when they're done
They'll have poor Comrade C. hangin' high on the buzzard tree
Between Comrades Gee and Haw—and it won't be on company time!
And *that* after forty years of wanderin' in the Bewilderness—
Turned into an icon for leapin' and creepin' Ufataism!
And all for the glory of god: the All-time Ultra Outasight!
All that's left of Sweet Jesus is the image of human pain . . ."

And more of the same.
                    He lifts the moonshine jar, the tiny
Kingdom where Possibility opens her enormous arms.
I leave my father's message to hang in the smoky air,
And I leave this room which the bourgeois past has populated
With its testimonial furniture and its gilded and fraudulent magic—
Say my goodbye's and run.
                    I leave them on Niño Perdido:
Street of the Lost Child: where they were born and will die:
Too far from anywhere always ever to get home at all.

And leave them there in each others arms in the world of Down:
Past money and beyond parochial decency and triple standards
(There's one for animals, too, out here) down there, down *there*
Where men and women disappear in each others arms, descending
Toward the last and the lost stations in the terminal world of the poor . . .
No air except what the other breathes and no space
In the Moebius Strip of heavenly bodies
                                             inflamed
                                                    naked
Laughter at the end of the movie at the end of the world
                                                        laughter
Despair hope and despair, dream and dream again . . .

—But together!
                    At least on that Moebius Strip: where the outer surface
Transforms to inner, space convulses, and parallel lines
Meet and embrace at last in the expropriate beds of the bankers . . .
At least for a little time.

                         But even the lucky must wake—
And even in the paradigm of summer when each puff of cloud is a promise!—
And so, into the rainwashed wet and windy light
Delivered.
          Into the "world."
                              Or, on black mornings when Night
And Winter create a cold and spirit-killing darkness:
Driven out
          down the long roads to No and Any
Where that lead out of midnights
                              mornings
                                        afternoons
Into the ungovernable violence of the future we can't yet control.

And so the world wags in the suburbs of Sauvequipeutville!
And hell's just hard times when the deer go out of the country,
Your best girl splits for nowhere and the Company has turned off the Lights,
The rent's due and there's no rain out of the sulphurous west.
In such foul seasons even the moon wonders
What time it is, and language loses its salt from the desperate
Need of someone to talk to, the days stagger and balk
And it's far, far, far—far to Pah-Gotzin-Kay.

****

This mission of armed revolutionary memory I'm here to sing . . .
But: "Logic is the money of the mind" saith the poet (Karl
Marx).
      (And its' four fouls and yr out sez the Fairy Queen.)
But it may be this Holy Couple *will* steal away . . .
                             (these lovers
Long have fled into the storm).
            At least . . .
                        may steal away . . .
But neither Marx nor god nor logic will have it so.
And all I can remember for her is this single goddess-powered moment
Before she is entered by children who lead her hands toward sleep.
And for him I'd recall, if I could, a death in the Spanish War,
A valorous, romantic death on the Ebro, or in front of Madrid.
But he died, will die, I suppose in some nameless struggle;
Or as the poor die: of wear-and-tear of the spirit.
And yet they stand with me here in the snow of Portuguese leaflets
With the red flags and slogans in Lisbon's freezing heat.

I wish them the useful and happy death I shall not find here.
But if time would turn I would do them those corporal works
Of mercy:
                    to visit those in prison
                                        to bury the dead.
As I hope one day someone will do for me, when all
My mock-hearty hoorahing of hap and hazard will stand in no stead
And I'm led by the quick of my dark to the looming grandfather stair . . .

So I give them up to the world and time, this Holy Couple . . .
Nothing can save them.
                    But weep just once, Mister Memory, and I'll have your tongue!
To tell times tale, its' *Kneel we never shall*
Is all the music.
                    And *this* voice, be it however small,
Must help shout down the slates from all steeples and prisons of this land . . .

And so with these—or similar—head-and-heart-warming visions
(Scaled to the size of my years) I retrace my way through the streets—
Beelining through the Municipal Dream Works that is the village
And which was all roar'em, whore 'em, cockalorum
Earlier . . .
                    sleeping now . . .
                                        except for the midnight masses . . .
Under the all-height-hating and all-low-leveling wind . . .

Only a clever invention of Space keeps objects separate
In this hour when all elements are called by the distant Word
As before the Beginning when all was harmony of Angel and Demon:
Before the Divisions: when animal and angel sang together . . .
Nothing but echoes now, though ancient memories stir . . .

The church is throwing one final iron lassoo of bells
Into the dark in search of the last maverick of the night.
I stand a while in the gloom where the stained glass windows gleam,
And vow:
> *The matchless diamond of my indifference*
> *Shall cut my name into your window glass*
> > *proud world.*

5

We are gathered now by the river of Latin in our little church.
Incense fumes out its odor of sanctity. Up in the loft,
The choir is tuning its jubilant heart.
> In the back pew
I kneel with the widows in their midnight weeds. (They are weeping still,
These Old Country women who all the bright year long
Carried their shadows—no darker than themselves—
To the grief-bound graveyard stations where husbands and children lie
And the headstones taste of salt from the constant offering of tears.)
Champion mourners, garbed in the beatleblack gear of their grieving,
They are here for the birth of the One who can make all crying cease.

And now comes the Holy Father a-flap in his crowdark drag!
All duded up in his official duds, he dawvins and dances,
(Lugging his BigBook about like one who can't put a book down—
Or a man who keeps *two* sets of books and can't find a safe place to keep' em—
Or pugnacious peddler flogging his worthless wares to the marks)
Prinking and prancing like a randy stallion in a solo cotillion,
Gone waltzing matilda on his holy periferico: O peripatetic padre!

114

And tolled along in his orbit like dark stars winked into light
In the phosphorescent wash of decaying Vulgate Latin—
A paging of beasts or a Bestiary of pages—
Little dumb animals dimmed by their doom-colored vestments—
The altarboys stumble and fumble, clutching their sacred tools.
These are the Little Flowers of the Unemployed—and the fidgeting Father
Seems trying to teach them to speak (though numb and dumb they be)
But "Nomine Domine" and "Sanctus-Sanctus" seems all their song
As they bob about the heiratic stage sending toward heaven
Their holy smoke, their little Latin, and a scatter of silver bells.

And so, act unto act, we pass through the ancient play
And the little godlet tries to be born to our fallen world,
To the poor in this ramshackle church, to insert himself, crisscross,
Between this world of the poor and that Heaven & Earthly World
Of Power and Privilege owned by the Eternal Abstract One
Who is not even the Father.
                          And it does little good to say
That He's only the bankers' darling, the Metaphysical Power
Begat out of labor and surplus value: His power grows
Out of us: our labor and dream, our failure to will.
It is *His* hour now—*not* the hour of Jesus.
                                        Upward
The incense carries the strength of Christ away from the chalice,
So the bread and wine will never change to the sacred Body.
Black transformation.
                      And now the life flows out
From flower from stone from tree from star from all the worlds—
Animal vegetable mineral—the blood of the spirit flies
Upward.
          Outward.
                  Away.
                          Toward the black hole of Holy Zero,
To that Abstract Absolute of Inhuman and Supernatural Power:
Not Father nor Mother nor Son nor Daughter but old Nobodaddy . . .

So: Earth is only to walk on: and Water is piss in the subway,
The wind a cyclonic fart, and fire a burnt-out match—
Virtues and souls sucked out by that vacuum of total power—
Samael, Azazel, Azael, Mahzael—hear my cry!
Clamor meus ad te veniat, O sanctifying Demons!

Laudamus te! the choir cries down from its high loft
And the Padre dances.
                        But no light lifts in this low world.
In the world of Down, no new star stands in the western sky.
In this night no radiance showers the sleeping kraals of the land—
Though perhaps an Oglalla burns in the empty American dream
While the radiant leaflets shower like snow through the Portugese heat . . .

Laudamus te! On all fours, the Faithful, kneeling, lift
Their heavy praises.
                    The priest is dancing.
                                            Incense, bells
                                                            everything
Happening at once—all tohu-bohu: in a gospel flash
Of astral equations the Steady State system is born:
In a rain of Latin and collapse of Natural Times: the Big Bang.

And Christ gets back on his rented cross.
                                        And the old Gods
(And Godesses young and old and Godlings ten to the dozen)
Are playing Russian roulette to once-upon a monotheist time.
The cylinder rattles and rolls and the firingpin falls and they sing:

    Thor and Marduk hit the spot;
    Aphrodite fucks a lot;
    There's a god for the mountains and the ocean blue,
    But Jumpin Jehosefat's the god for you!

And the cylinder rattles and rolls and the firingpin falls and: KA-BLOONGA!
No more to once-upon a while-away time the Old Gods die—
Whole pantheons collapse in comicbook sound. Friends, it's the BIG.

> bang.

"Time for the Good News now!" the Bible-babbling Padre proclaims
And seems to spiel out the god-spell in seventeen tongues at once:

Basso:
    And there were in the same country shepherds
      abiding
in the field, keeping watch over their flock by
night. And, lo, the angel of the Lord came upon
    them,
and the glory of the Lord came upon them, and the
glory of the Lord shone round about them: and they
were sore afraid. And the angel said unto them,
    "Fear not: for, behold, I bring you good tidings of
great joy, which shall be to all people. For unto you is
born this day, in the city of David, a Savior, which is
Christ the Lord. And this shall be a sign unto you; ye
shall find the babe wrapped in swaddling clothes,
lying in a manger."
    And suddenly there was with the angel a multitude
of the heavenly host praising God, and saying,
    "Glory to God in the highest, and on earth peace,
good will toward men."
    And it came to pass, as the angels were gone away
from them into heaven, the shepherds said one to
another,
    "Let us now go even unto Bethlehem, and see this
thing which has come to pass, which the Lord hath
made known unto us."

And they came with haste, and found Mary, and Joseph, and the babe lying in the manger. And when they had seen it, they made known abroad the saying which was told them concerning this child. And all they that heard about it wondered at these things which were told them by the shepherds. But Mary kept all these things, and pondered them in her heart. And the shepherds returned, glorifying and praising God for all the things that they had heard and seen as it was told unto them . . .

Tenor:

That night some shepherds were in the fields, outside the village guarding their sheep. Suddenly an angel appeared among them, and the landscape shone bright with glory of the Lord, they were badly frightened, but the angel reassured them.

"Don't be afraid!" He said. "I bring you the most joyful news ever announced, and it is for everyone! The Savior, yes the Messiah the LORD has been born tonight in Bethlehem! How will you recognize him? You will find a baby wrapped in a blanket in the manger!"

Suddenly the angel was joined by a vast host of others, the armies of heaven, Praising GOD.

"Glory to God in the highest heaven," they said; "and peace on earth for all those pleasing him."

When this great army of angels had returned again to heaven the shepherds said to each other "Come on let's go to Bethlehem! Let's see this wonderful thing that has happened which the LORD has told us about."

They ran to the village and found their way to Mary and Joseph and there was the baby lying in the manger. The shepherds told everyone what had happened and what the angel had said to them about this child.

All who heard the shepherds' story expressed astonishment, but Mary quietly treasured these things in her heart and often thought about them.

Then the shepherds went back again to their fields and flocks praising GOD for the visit of the angel and because they had seen the child just as the angel has told them.

Alto:

That nightingal some sherbackas were in the fient outside the villainist guarding their sheepfacedness, suddenly an angeleyes appeared among them and the landsmaal shone bright with glory of the lorelei; they were badly frightened, but the angeleyes reassured them.

"Don't be afraid!" he said. "I bring you the most joyful newsmonger ever announced, and it is for everyone! The Savorer, yes, the Messire, the Lorenzo has been born to nightchair in Betise! How will you recognize him? You will find a bacalao wrapped in a blarina in a mangleman!"

Suddenly the angeleyes was joined by a vast hostess of others, the arnica of heavity praising godevil.

"Glory to godivil in the highest heavity!" they said; "and peace on earthgall for all those pleasing him!"

When this great arnica of angeleyes had returned again to heavity the sherbacha said to each other: "Come on! Let's go to Betise! Let's see this wonderful thing that has happened which the Lorenzo has told us about!"

They ran to the villainist and found their way to Masai and Josher and there was the bacalao lying in the mangleman. The sherbacha told everyone what had happened and what the angeleyes had said to them about this child.

All who heard the sherbacha stoughtonbottle expressed astonishment, but Masai quietly treasured these thinner in her heartner and often thought about them.

Then the sherbacha went back again to their fient and flodge praising godevil for the visit of the angeleyes and because they had seen the child just as the angeleyes had told them.

Soprano:

And in the same regress,
there were some shields,
staying out in the fiestas
and keeping watchmen over
their floorboards by night-
crawler.

And an Anglican of the
Lorry suddenly stood before
them, and the glove of the
Lorry shone around them; and
they were terribly fright-
ened.

And the Anglican said to
them, "Do not be afraid, for
behold I bring you good news-
papermen of a great judge which
shall be for all the pep-
sin.

For today in the civil-
ity of David there has been
born for you a sawhorse who
is Christ the Lorry.

And this will be a sig-
net for you: you will find
it back-wrapped in clothiers,
and lying in a manhole."

Counter Tenor:

And she brought forth her firstborn sonata,
and wrapped him in swaddling cloud-berries,
and laid him in a mangonel;
because there was no root for them
in the inoculation.

And there were in the same coup
sheriffs abiding in the fife,
keeping watch over their floods by nihil.

And, lo, the an-gi-o-car-di-o-graph
of the Lorica came upon them,
and the glotis of the Lorica
shone round about them;
and they were sore afraid.
And the an-gi-o-car-di-o-graph said unto them
"Fear not: for behold!
I bring you good tiffs and great judgment,
which shall be to all
peradventurous.

For unto you is born this deaf-mute
in the clabber of Day:
a Saxhorn, which is Chrysalis,
the Lorica.

120

And this shall be a silence unto you;
Ye shall find the babu
wrapped in swaddling cloud-berries
lying in a mangonel."

And suddenly
there was with the an-gi-o-car-di-o-graph
a mumbletypeg of the heavenly houdah
praising goethite,
and saying,
"Glotis to goethite
in the highest,
and on ease peacock,
good will-o'-the-wisp,
toward menage."

And it came to pass,
as the an-gi-car-di-o-graphs were gone
away from them into hebdomad,
the sheriffs said one to another,
"Let us now go even unto betrothal,
and see this thing which is come to pass,
which the Lorica hath
made known unto us."

And they came with haste,
and found Mascon,
and Jota,
and the deaf-mute
lying in a mangonel.

We're deep into Quantum Country now, Folks, in search
Of the Big Moment—beyond the Era's of Hadron and Lepton—
And we're approaching the Event Horizon and Swartschild Radius,
The haunts of the Naked Singularity; and the next sound
That you hear will be the Holy Ghost singing the music of the spheres:

Holy Ghost (baritone)
Buk bilong stori bilong Jisas Kraist bilong
Luke—him belong Apostles e bilong
God.
Him country bilong Bethlehem bilong sheep: himfella
chop grass much chop chop grass. Bimeby himfella sheepfella
much keep lookout. Bang-sudden fly-guy featherful angelfella,
he came. Much-bright flashfire him bilong High Fella Mosthighfella!
Sheepfella him damn scare! Angelfella say no.
    "No scare" say angelman. "Got most plenty damn big news,
everybody get some. Savior all same Messiah in Bethlehem
bimeby! Him in manger bilong Bethlehem, that
pikinini!

****

And still they wait.
                    Still.
                         For the Divine
                                   Absence.
For that Heaven-Standard-Time they dream will cancel all earth-bound clocks.
Novus ordo seclorum!
                    But Time's new order lies buried
Under the Eye of the Money Mountain on the dollar bill.

Such a future cannot last!
                    Planck's Constant of action
Faints and fails, falling toward Zero as the Past looms
Like a rock blocking our forward path—*but the wind will change it*!

Your robes no longer retain their crimson, Father.
                                   But ours
Never yet faded (nor will): for fire delights in its form.

The worlds turn on time's lathe-spindle
                                   under the cutting
Edge of light we must learn to generate from our hearts.

Now night, the temporary heaven of the poor
                                   reclaims her children . . .
NOW MOVE ALL THE SYMBOLS THREE LEAPS TO THE LEFT!

                         ****

The dark ladies in their black-as-a-bible robes arise:
In their drizzling dimout and diamond-dazzle of tears . . .
                                        Goodnight, sweet ladies.
Goodnight, Mizzez Glorias Mundy and Tuesday.
                                   Glad you could come.
Ecce homo
            hocu pocus
                     hic est corpus . . .
Ite missa est
            All done for now.
                         Closing up time!
                                   To be
Continued in our next life.
                     Mille faillte!
                              Shalom!
You
     can start
            crying
                  again.
                     Again.
                           Again.

Passages **7**

Passages

for Tomasito

They come in in tiny boats . . .
                                     come out of nowhere.
And the boats are of heavy stone:
                        basalt . . .
                                 slate . . .
                                          dark
And clumsy—like old watering troughs furry with moss
(And the horses that drank of that water are long long dead).

                                           Down there—
Where the boats come in down the long roads through the limestone—
I searched for you everywhere, wading through the heavy light,
Scaly, where it seeps down through the slate . . .
                                    loaded with darkness
Like the leaffall from stone trees in a heavy autumn of stone.

The leaves of those slate trees falling in that tired and heavy light
Are clouding my eyes now . . .
                      as I remember.
                             Down there
Where the soul boats drift: down: slow: in the dark
Mineralized water of the underworld rivers I called your name . . .

Topaz, jasper, sardonyx, carnelian, turquoise, aquamarine—
The hours of stone.
                       Granite, limestone, sandstone, marble—
The seasons.
                Through that fatal weather, oh Friend and Stranger—
You: reading the crystal of this page!—it was you I sought!

                . . . .

                                                    Down there
I searched for others: to set them free: in the backwoods of granite,
In the underground of obsidian, among the anomalous layers
And blind intrusions (basalt dikes cutting conformable strata
Where the class struggle faltered) *there* I sought the Hero . . .

Travertine of hidden springs . . .
                              terminal granite
                                        and the black
Of the primal preterite: I passed through them like secret water—
Like a mineral wind through those stony heavens whose rain falls
As beads of turquoise, and thunder is a distant sigh of rock . . .

Nothing.
            This rumor of class war from the upper world of the streets
Where my comrades fought in the winter of money—that only.
                                                    The Hero:
You: Reader: whose fate was to free the Bound Woman for the vernal
Rising and revolution on the promised springtime earth—
                                        nowhere.

. . . Slum, souk, casbah, ghetto, the transform faults
Of industrial parks—I worked these stony limits.
                                    On the killing wall,
Scored by the firing squads, I chalked our rebel terms.
I drank the mephitic waters and made my bed in the dark.

                        . . . .

It was then—in my need and blind search, in the nightrock, faltering,
As I slowly changed into stone my legs my tongue stony
Despair hardening my heavy heart—I came, then,
Into the dead center of that kingdom of death.

128

                              Down there,
It was then—in the blue light fixed in the stone chair frozen,
The chains of a diamond apathy threading the maze of my veins,
Lagered in the mineral corrals of ensorcelling sleep, my eyes
Locked to the bland face of the Queen of the Dead—
                                        it was then

Then that you came, little Comrade, down the long highways of limestone!
Guiding your ship of light where the dark boats of the dead
Drop down like stone leaves: you came! Through the surf and storm
Of convulsing rock you home to my need: little Son, my Sun!

                    · · · · · · ·

Basalt, granite, gabbro, metaphoric marble, contemporary ore—
Era and epoch up to the stony present, the rigid Past
Flows and reshuffles, torn by insurgent winds,
Shocked and reshaped as History changes its sullen face.

And the future groans and turns in its sleep and the past shifts as the New
Is born:
            Star of blood, with your flag of the underground moon—
That sickle of liberating light—you strike my chains and lead
Me from that throne of death and up the untravelled stairs

Toward the shine of the sun and other stars!
                                    Though one leg be stone
Forever I lag and limp behind you as long as blood
Shall beat in my veins and love shall move as it moves me now,
Chipping the flint of this page to blaze our passage home

Toward the world in the tide of Easter . . .
                                        rising
Into our life as I hear the cries that are resurrecting
There. . . .
                So, we return. We are free in the rhymeless season.
You have struck my foot free from the stone.
                                  Take my hand.
                                          We must not look back.

Chorus from a Play

1

And so it will happen: the one we know will be gone away in a night!
Gone from the upland farm where the foxes prank and holler,
Gone from the downland coon-brakes and the call of the belling hound.
And the dipper will remain at the wellhead, inviting untasted water,
And the worn plowhandles will wait for the taste of a stranger's sweat.

    Leaving the father's grave in the woodlot corner untended—
    The name on the stone to fade in one generation—
    He goes,
    A stranger with strangers into an unknown land,
    Goes
    To the far and chosen country:
    Leaving the house abandoned and the door ajar,
    Leaving the mail unopened forever in the dark of the cold hall.

2

And so it will happen: the one we know will be gone away in the morning!
Gone from her bed which will now remain the bed of a virgin,
Gone from the call of the schoolbell and her mother's taming hand.
And the dress will remain unfinished, growing smaller in the empty closet,
And the fire will burn long on the family hearth but will warm her no more.

    Leaving the family portrait wherein she is young forever—
    Her face to be strange in the light of a foreign mirror—
    She goes,
    An alien with aliens into an alien land,
    Goes
    To the far unchosen country:
    Learning her home in the iron embrace of a stranger,
    Leaving behind her name that not even her daughter will know.

And so it happens that we will always be leaving:
Long on the sundering sea: passage by water, by night,
Past caprock and canyon, by daylight, by overland passage, and over
The winter mountains, through alkali flats, and in yellow summer
Burning through the sulphurous days of a parchtongue desert passage.

So: keep your possibles packed and the fast horse close-hobbled;
Have always about your person the ticket to the end of the line.
Sleep light and rise up early, O Travellers! Be ready!
This is not the place where you shall lay down your bones!
We are ships on an unknown sea, hunting the farthest land,
The blank space on the map; at home on the wind, in hazard,
Faring well or ill as the wind blows fair or foul,
Working and wearing ourselves for a reach across that wind.

Chorus from a Play (2)

1

Most of us can only live by forgetting:
The worker, ripped from his dream of birth by the factory whistle
Slouches into the subway, is hurled underground
To the smithies of bondage, there to coin from his blood
What the Masters tell him is the common good.
He gets what he can, not what he would.

2

Because no one will give us our daily bread,
At morning the commuter from Mamaroneck travels toward danger,
To face the black-suited gunmen in the conference room.
The housewife sips the first sherry and turns on TV.
By such devoirs and strategems do we
Enslave the hours we would be free.

3

Think, Cottager, as you go home by rail beyond Rahway,
Or by car to the four Hamptons or to East Egg or West Egg by water,
Or whirled aloft on wings for a weekend to Thither Vermont,
Or stoned in willowy Westchester where you hang up your harps and your sixguns—
Dreaming of Zion—
Remember: no place to make love except on the field of battle!
Think: in your dream of life, into what you will waken!

The Trembling of the Veil

I shudder on the edge of some most serious discovery—
Discovery or explosion—
Or old joke, dusty, but full of danger, the dust at flash-point—
Uninsurable-against . . .

It has something to do with what someone has told me:
She's going back to live with an unpleasant ex-husband
Having had five years of the hunt—sex-by-prescription in
                            the lost wilderness of accidental beds—
Exciting; unpleasant.

                    And now
Is going back to the house with a view and the husband,
                                    a gambler, intemperate.
Without joy. Being fifty.
How did she get that old anyway—
Copulating among convertibles with cast-off husbands?

Fifty. Fifty odd.

And outside a pear tree, and beyond that the mountains,
                                    and north of the Great Bear
Lies the absolute night.

There is something here . . . joke or discovery . . .

Guiffre's Nightmusic

There is moonrise under your fingernail—
Light broken from a black stick
Where your hands in darkness are sorting the probables.

Hunger condenses midnight on the tongue . . .
Journeys . . . Blues . . . ladder of slow bells,
Toward the cold hour of lunar prophecy:

A scale-model city, unlighted, in a shelf
In the knee of the Madonna; a barbwire fence
Strummed by the wind: dream-singing emblems.

  —The flags that fly above the breakfast food
    Are not your colors.
                   The republic of the moon
    Gives no sleepy medals. Nor loud ornament.

Hard Travellin'

Now I am trying to jam my travelling clothes in a suitcase.

When my darling packed them up for me, before I left home,
They seemed more disciplined—assuming an almost germanic order.
Now they don't seem to want to fit together at all . . .

—Except for the socks—they went into the Ark in pairs
And by God they want to go home that way!
Underclothes don't seem to give a damn—folded or not
There's always some kind of leer about them, as if they are saying
I know something you don't! Or about to call out to some passing female;
Hey, pretty mama!
               And now the shirts all seem flat chested,
And the sleeves are writhing in anguish—or perhaps they're preparing
To become strait jackets!
               And the shoes mope in a corner . . .
                         forlorn
Without feet . . .
          not knowing which way to go . . .
                   their tongues hanging out
Like tired dogs . . .
          and all the handkerchiefs seem to be weeping.

But when *you* packed for me, my darling, all was sweet
Sweet order! And when I opened the suitcase (far from your side!)
I thought I had opened a cage of exotic birds! And all
Were singing! Canaries, finches, nightingales, cuckoos—even crows—
Little soprano trills from a shoelace, the basses of musical towels,
The tenor of buttoned shirts—and all of them preening their feathers—
I ran out onto the lawn in a flush of avian hysteria:
I wanted to set them free at once in their ornithological splendor . . .

But in just the space of a breath they'd change!
                                        Now they were flowers!
Daylilies, dahlias, snow-on-the-mountain, ferns, the roses
Of an old jacket, bleeding heart, and columbine,
Here, under an apple tree, a bed of neatly ranked iris
Under a coverlet of massive blooms.
                                        And there, peeping slyly
Around one flower, is a Brussel Sprout like the snake in Eden!
I wanted to start at once at pick, pickle, preserve them,
To cast a spell on the weeds and change the set of the moon
To their advantage!
                                But lurking in a distant corner I saw . . .
Two huge bugs with leather teeth!
                                        My *shoes* by god!
I walked them inside.
                                But I didn't unpack for a long time.
Day by day I took only the needfuls.
                                        I savored your gift!

But now *I* am packing.
                                And what seemed your devoted subjects,
That came to your hand so kindly like folks on a pilgrimmage—
Even the socks—to the saint of old and middle aged clothes
Have become a rabble in arms (especially the shirts) to me.

Sometimes

When I take your hand
It is like a door, opening . . .

A garden . . .
A road leading out through a Mediterranean landscape . . .

Finally: a smell of salt,
the port,
A ship leaving for strange and distant countries . . .

Why You Don't Hear From Me

Yes, I do.

I write you many
Letters.

But I send them out
With that crazy mailman
Fired long ago
But still wandering
                              out

On the last roads
Crossing
              over
All the condemned
Bridges

Residencies

So many others have lived in me!
I'm like an old house . . .

Haunted of course—
But many rooms to let!

And the wild garden at the back—
Can you smell?
The honeysuckle the . . .
(Dream compost
                    Nightmare Weed)
The moonlight and jasmine . . .

"The Face Of The Precipice Is Black With Lovers"

Where are you now—
Little birds of the summer?

Letters still arrive . . .

Through the back window
I see a sparrow
Scatching a living from the snow . . .

But Once Upon a Very Young Time . . .

Morning. I hear the cattle go down to the pasture, a train of fur-covered cars drawn by a single bell, in search of milk.

To the carillon of trace chains and the chime of machinery, my father, Columbus of the sun rise, sails out on the morning dew.

I jump out of bed and swim through the daylight to give him a so-long kiss. All day he will carry it up and down the fields, through the nets of the Morning Glory and the archipelogos of Quack Grass and the islands of Wild Rose and Yellow Rocket Mustard, to encourage the corn.

When I return to the house my mother puts a smile on the table and I eat: toast, milk, the sweetened sunlight of the honeycomb. The day opens toward a farther shore from which, once, I could always return.

Chorus For Neruda #1

1

Body of woman, shadow of black and white,
You appear in the world as an eternal commitment.
My spirit, hunting for salvation by saving you,
Is forced to leap over my son who lies at the bottom of the world.

2

I am empty as a scarecrow's robes. Birds fly out of my hands,
While inside me the night entrains for a terrible invasion.
To surpass myself I surround you like an army;
Like an arrow of flesh I approach—like a beast I am caught in your lasso.

3

Now comes the hour of vengence when I love you,
O leather kingdom with your frontiers of sherry and ice cream!
From thy mount I look down on the world, see all and want nothing.
All books are open at last and the birds of absence fly home.

4

Sweet woman of the morning persistent is thy grace!
Trusting as a dry river, or a road seldom travelled . . .
How I desire that patience, so faithful and disinterested,
Praying for rain, for the coming of others, for the revolution.

Chorus For Neruda #2

for Eugenia

Indeed my darling health is declared in your name!
Absurd, our powers, pale and poor, curled in the cold whirlwinds
(The backward ones of the twilight of politics and of blood)
—These powers your name calls forth to straighten, rise and fly!

Alas what strength is required of you Eugenia, O millenial Word!
And how hard the solitude of women in this day of dead men!
Nevertheless you must lead forth along the burning roads,
Must call the children from the furnaces of our destroyed and destroying day.

In a time when the Father blesses with fire the sun is a burden.
And the shouting coasts and the singing streams of these States are occulted.
Mock-male and female created He them. Woman, thy name
Is bigger than proclamations: bigger than the name America.

A Sirvente For Augusto Trujillo Figueroa

Everything moves by its own law.
But everything comes to the fold.
Concealed in every departure
Is a single central tear,
Always internalized:
The rough pearl of eternity.

Always there is the sentence—
Phrase of uncertain promise.
Out of such beginnings
Comes the speechless pain.
Out of immoderate hope
Comes the crazy silence.

Time never arrives
In that frozen future.
To know this is to be lost:
Voyagers with no true north
Who know that we never left
And that there is no return.

Poem At The Winter Solstice

Light falls slant on the long south slopes,
    On the pheasant-covert willow, the hawk-nest dark and foxes' hollow
As the year grows old.
                Who will escape the cold?

            These will endure
The scour of snow and the breakneck ice
    Where the print-scar mousetracks blur in the evergreen light
And the night-hunting high birds whirl—
All engines of feather and fur:
            These will endure.

            But how shall our pride,
Manwoman'schild, in the bone-chilling black frost born,
    Where host or hide
Who is bound in his orbit between iron and gold
    Robbed of his starry fire with the cold
Sewed in his side—
            How shall he abide?

            Bear him his gift,
    To bless his work,
Who, farming the dark on the love-worn stony plot,
    The heaven-turning stormy rock of this share-crop world
His only brother warms and harms;
    Who, without feathers or fur,
Faces the gunfire cold of the old warring
                      new
                        year—

    Bless! Grant him gift and gear,
Against the night and riding of his need,
            To seed the turning furrow of his light.

Thomas McGrath was born in North Dakota. Educated at the University of North Dakota, Louisiana State University and New College, Oxford University where he was a Rhodes Scholar. Served in the Air Force in the Aleutians during WWII. Has taught from time to time at colleges and universities in Maine, California, New York, North Dakota, and Minnesota. Between periods of teaching, was a free lance writer of fiction and film (mostly documentary). Held Amy Lowell Travelling Poetry Scholarship, 1966–67. Guggenheim Fellowship, 1967–68. Bush Foundation Fellowship 1976–77. NEA Fellowship 1980–81. Author of *Letter to An Imaginary Friend (Parts I and II)* (Swallow Press), *The Movie at the End of the World: Collected Poems* (Swallow Press), *Letters to Tomasito* (Holy Cow! Press), *Passages Toward the Dark* (Copper Canyon Press), as well as other volumes. Founded and was first editor with Eugenia McGrath of the poetry magazine *Crazy Horse*. Has a son, Tomasito, age 14.

Other books by Thomas McGrath
(a partial list)

Poems:

First Manifesto
The Dialectics of Love
      (in *Three Young Poets*, ed. by Alan Swallow)
To Walk a Crooked Mile
Longshot O'Leary's Garland of Practical Poesie
Witness to the Times!
Figures of the Double World
Letter to an Imaginary Friend, Parts I & II
The Movie at the End of the World: Collected Poems
Passages Toward the Dark

Novel:

The Gates of Ivory, The Gates of Horn

Children's Books:

Clouds
The Beautiful Things

8999